Getting Started with OpenVMS™ System Management

Getting Started with OpenVMS™ System Management

David Donald Miller

dp

Digital Press
An imprint of Elsevier Science

Amsterdam • Boston • London • New York • Oxford • Paris • San Diego
San Francisco • Singapore • Sydney • Tokyo

Library of Congress Cataloging-in-Publication Data
Miller, David Donald.
    Getting started with open VMS system management / Dave Miller.
       p. cm.
    ISBN: 1-55558-281-8
    1. OpenVMS 2. Operating systems (Computers) I. Title

QA76.76.O63 M5615 2003
005.4'32–dc21

                                        2002041321

British Library Cataloguing-in-Publication Data
A catalogue record for this book is available from the British Library.

The publisher offers special discounts on bulk orders of this book.
For information, please contact:

Manager of Special Sales
Elsevier Science
200 Wheeler Road
Burlington, MA 01803
Tel: 781-313-4700
Fax: 781-313-4882

For information on all Digital Press publications available, contact our World Wide Web home page at: http://www.digitalpress.com or http://www.bh.com/digitalpress

Transferred to Digital Printing 2006

Table of Contents

Appendix B – VMS and the Web   145

By Alan Winston

Appendix C – Assessing OpenVMS and Linux: The Right Tool for the Right Job   153

By John Robert Wisniewski

Appendix D – Memory Management System Services   161

By Ruth E. Goldenberg

Appendix E – Symbols, Data, and Expressions   171

By Paul C. Anagnostopoulos and Steve Hoffman

Acknowledgments

This book is Pam Chester's (an acquisition editor for Digital Press) idea, and I am very happy she asked me to do it. Theron R. Shreve, Pam's boss, also had a lot of input in formulating this book. Pam and Theron have been patient with my tardiness and relentless questions about the mechanics of the publishing business. In case you have not kept up, publishing has changed enormously in the last 10 years. In 1990 manuscripts were submitted in hard copy via FedEx and authors reviewed galley proofs. Now the manuscript is electronic and e-mails fly back and forth.

Thanks, too, to Alan Rose and Tim Donar for transforming, magically it seems, my manuscript into a real, live book. I really have no appreciation for all that is required and, frankly, do not want to be bothered with the details.

Also a great big "THANKS" to all the contributors to the comp.os.vms (COV) news group. I'm sorry there are too many individuals to name, and I hesitate to single any out because I may offend the others. COV discussions get my juices running and help me to focus on the important system management issues. The discussions are an endless source of information, both current and historical. Additionally, I had to post a few questions from time-to-time, just to clarify my thinking. The answers I received were thoughtful and complete every time. I have never been made to feel stupid when I received an answer, even if (in retrospect) the question was stupid. Thanks folks!

My two reviewers, Sue Rosselet of Bemidji State University and Helen Johnson, were great. The whole concept of the book changed as we worked together. As a result they read various forms of the manuscript three times. Such fortitude! Such dedication! Such patience! What a team!

Finally, thanks to my patient wife, Kari. She makes life go on when I do not have a life – when my life is a keyboard. She forces me to take time out and take her out, which is thoroughly enjoyable once I am able to unglue my eyes from the screen. And she is unbelievably patient with the mess; the books, manuals, e-mail printouts and bits of stickies everywhere. Thanks honey!

David Miller
Green Valley, Arizona
November, 2002.

Preface

Why OpenVMS? You've been assigned to learn OpenVMS and you don't know a thing about it. Here is a short list of features.

- The external documentation is excellent and much of it is on the Internet in both .pdf and .html format. Check out www.openvms.compaq.com:8000/.

- The internal documentation via the $HELP command is probably the best in the industry. Online displays discuss errors in a way that no other system does.

- OpenVMS commands are English-like and options for one command are also valid for others.

- For programmers, it has a great debugger. The debugger will operate in either a command line mode or in a GUI mode for Motif users.

- OpenVMS includes a robust file system which includes indexed files.

- The backup utility can handle tape errors very well. Files that are backed up are time-stamped.

- OpenVMS is one of the most secure systems available. At a recent hackers convention, the attendees declared it unhackable.

- There are no viruses known that affect OpenVMS.

- System performance is seriously supported with a number of tools. Documentation included detailed algorithms to guide you in their use.

- The discussion group, comp.os.vms, is one of the helpful and active. Newbies are always welcome.

- The FAQ on Internet is at www.openvms.compaq.com/wizard /openvms_faq.html and is actively maintained.

- Many OpenVMS users also maintain informational sites, for instance www.levitte.org/~ava/.

- Compaq/HP supports a hobby program offering free licenses for OpenVMS and many layered products. See details at www.montagar.com/hobbyist. Several third party suppliers also have hobby programs.

- Patches for many versions of OpenVMS and layered products are available at ftp.support.compaq.com/public/vms.

A system manager has to be multi-lingual these days. You must be conversant in several operating systems to do the job right. But learning and keeping track of them all can be a daunting task. Certainly keeping details on the tip of your tongue is not easy and there is never enough time to look up specifics or research the details. So I have put the essentials of OpenVMS management in an easy-to-reference form. I have collected the most common operations and tools together in one place. Then I included references to the Compaq/HP manuals and other books that you will need to finish the job. I did it this way because if I included the detailed instructions I'd be merely duplicating already published references. I thought that by concisely encapsulating this key information in a smallish book, you, the system manager, could easily and quickly find what you're looking for. In fact, the mere mention of a particular tool or data structure might be just the hint you need to continue your task without resorting to the detailed description.

Conversely, this book is not intended to stand alone. It is incomplete in that many commands are simply not mentioned. Of those that are, only a few of the many options are discussed. You cannot manage a system with this resource alone.

A second reason for writing this book is to introduce a UNIX or Windows system manager to OpenVMS without a lot of effort. There is just enough in this book to see how Windows NT, UNIX, and OpenVMS are related; what additional features are supported by OpenVMS and, perhaps, what features are missing. With the information provided, a system manager can easily locate the specifics required to achieve a certain goal without detailed knowledge of the manuals and books that are available. But this is done without attempting to present a self-contained resource. If you need to know how to translate a particular UNIX grep command into an equivalent OpenVMS $SEARCH command, you will have to do that research yourself.

This is the third purpose of this book. From time to time questions from students or job seekers are published on comp.os.vms, the primary OpenVMS list about OpenVMS overviews. This book outlines the essential capabilities and operations of OpenVMS without subjecting the reader to detailed explanations of each and every required step. The reader can quickly and easily peruse the key capabilities of OpenVMS to gain a basic level of expertise in a short time.

But this is not a step-by-step how-to-manage book. Instead it introduces several areas of OpenVMS system management and describes why each is important and how it fits into the larger management task. I only included minimal examples because this book is intended to be a precursor to *OpenVMS System Management Guide* by Baldwin[1].

However I do name key data files and tool names (scripts and programs) so the reader can relate this book to other manuals and texts.

I will refer the reader to OpenVMS manuals published by Compaq/HP, books from Digital Press and books from other publishers. Compaq/HP documentation is voluminous and extremely detailed. I have tried to identify the best place the reader can find additional information for a given topic and I include a URL for the primary sites although that may change with the merger. From time to time I point out other information about OpenVMS that is available via the Internet, particularly user supported freeware sites.

When I started writing this book, OpenVMS 7.3 was well established and was my source of information. However, before I was finished, OpenVMS 7.3-1 was released and with it, updated manuals. I decided to complete the manuscript with 7.3 as the resource, so if I have missed a important new feature, I apologize in advance. Both documentation sets are available at the same location.

Even though some OpenVMS management concepts are unique (for instance user quotas) many concepts (such as account creation) have counterparts in UNIX and Windows NT. So, wherever possible the parallel to other systems will be pointed out to the reader.

The audience for this text would be UNIX and Windows NT system managers that are transitioning to OpenVMS system management. This book can also target system manager wannabes who have no experience and who are approaching OpenVMS for the first time. I've been told that OpenVMS is the easiest of all systems to manage. Of course this is a subjective opinion and can start all sorts of arguments. Regardless of the validity of my opinion, if you are a manager new to OpenVMS, be prepared for a very different management interface.

Communication with OpenVMS is via commands entered at a shell (borrowing a UNIX term) prompt, which is a dollar sign. The shell is called DCL (Digital Command Language or DEC Command Language), and unlike UNIX, there is only one supported shell language. The commands are more English-like than UNIX; TYPE not cat, DIRECTORY not ls and HELP not man. The command interpreter (like the UNIX shell) is more forgiving; abbreviations are accepted, it is case insensitive, and for the most part command arguments are position independent. However, Motif is supported by OpenVMS and other X-Windows managers have been ported as well so it is possible that a user may never need to learn much about DCL. The manager will have to learn DCL however. Even so, there are some MS Windows and Motif management tools available from Compaq/HP and from the user community.

---

1. A second edition of the Management Guide, by Baldwin, Hoffman and Miller, is planned.

My intention is to make brevity the primary feature of this text. Experienced system managers that do not have scads of time to spend on the extensive formal documentation can find out what they need to know, then jump into the specific management task. So, this book is intended to be a quick start to OpenVMS system management concepts with brief examples.

The book is divided into ten chapters, one for each of the most important system management tasks. Each chapter covers

- A definition of the management task.

- Several examples of what needs to be done using specific OpenVMS commands.

- Some references to manuals and documents. There is also an annotated bibliography following chapter 10 which contains the detailed citations.

- A summary of the pertinent commands and key files involved in the topic.

Online Course

OpenVMS Primer for System Managers located at www.openvms.compaq. com/wbt/pc/welcome.htm might be a useful place for a novice to start. This is a DCL course, primarily. Other DCL helps are found in the bibliography.

Conventions

Within a paragraph both acronyms and DCL commands are capitalized. The reader should be able to distinguish between the two. A sample command sequence is listed together with the resulting output separated from the prose, and monospaced. That will look somewhat like a screen display, for instance

```
$ INITIALIZE/QUEUE/BATCH -
_$ /AUTOSTART_ON=(NODE1::, NODE2::)   SYS$BATCH
```

The dash at the right end of the first line is typed by the user and indicates the command is continued on the next line. The second line's prompt is '_$' not '$' to indicate the continuation.

Organization

I have organized this book in roughly the same order that Baldwin laid out the OpenVMS System Management Guide; however, mine is written in a higher level of detail. Since this may be the reader's first exposure to OpenVMS, I start my book with a history of Digital Equipment Corporation, Compaq Computer Corporation, and Hewlett-Packard, the three companies that have supported the OpenVMS operating system.

I also thought a brief introduction to the VAX and Alpha hardware architecture and the history of both computers would helpful since OpenVMS is intertwined with the hardware hosts. Incidentally, some versions of UNIX will run on both the VAX and the Alpha hardware. There is an Alpha version of Linux available and Windows NT was supported on the Alpha at one time.

The reader will find a rather unusual feature in the Appendices. As I mentioned, since this may be the reader's first exposure to OpenVMS, I decided to include excerpts of five OpenVMS-related Digital Press publications – each one is about ten pages long. This is not blatant advertising but proof that OpenVMS is supported outside Compaq/HP corporate umbrella and that helpful books beyond the company manuals are available.

I included these five so that you may get a flavor for the breadth, style and content of these other publications. Notice, that I did not simply include Chapter 1 from each book. Rather I carefully selected a chapter that represented the subject of the particular book so the you might get a better idea of the author's level of detail. Unfortunately these books are not available at your local bookstore so you can not run out and look them over. However, you can find them at the online bookstores and at www.bhusa.com/digitalpress.

Related Publications

1. UNIX-based administrators may want to consult *UNIX for OpenVMS Users, Second Edition*, by Philip Bourne, Richard Holstein, and Joseph McMullen from Digital Press. The title implies that you must know VMS to learn UNIX but I think the book can be used in the opposite sense as well.

2. Windows NT-based administrators may want to look at *Windows NT for OpenVMS Professionals* by David Solomon published by Digital Press. Like the UNIX book above it can be used to relate Windows NT commands to OpenVMS.

3. No matter what your background, *The OpenVMS User's Guide* is probably a good investment too. It describes the basics of using OpenVMS, its primary commands and tools.

4. The comp.os.vms discussion group is mirrored on INFO-VAX, a list server. To subscribe to INFO-VAX, send e-mail to INFO-VAX-REQUEST@mvb.saic.com with the message SUBSCRIBE INFO-VAX. This is a very active list with around 100 messages posted per day. Like any list, not all messages pertain to OpenVMS technical discussions though.

5. All online documentation is rooted at www.openvms.compaq.com:8000. This page contains links for OpenVMS manuals for several versions. Some manuals are only available in HTML others in PDF and many in both formats. Of course the documents are available from Compaq/HP in hard copy and CD formats as well.

The OpenVMS Version 7.3 New Features and Documentation Overview includes a section describing all the manuals available from Compaq, including order numbers.

Chapter 1 — Introduction

- OpenVMS today

- A brief history of Digital/Compaq/HP

- A brief history of OpenVMS

- OpenVMS concepts: A brief tutorial

According to Compaq/HP literature, OpenVMS (virtual memory system) is installed on more than 450,000 computers worldwide and has more than 10 million users. This installed base includes five of the top ten stock exchanges and more than 50 other exchanges and clearinghouses. More than 80 percent of the automated lotteries are run on OpenVMS machines; 90 percent of the world's CPU chips are manufactured on assembly lines that are monitored and controlled by OpenVMS. Northern Light's Web search engine is the largest text-retrieval database in the history of the world, and it runs on OpenVMS. The largest, fastest mail list server in the world (1.3 million deliveries per hour and more than 6 million deliveries per day) is powered by OpenVMS. More than 80 million customers for the largest mobile communications company are billed with an OpenVMS-supported system.

OpenVMS is a solid and mature product designed and built by Digital Equipment Corporation in the late 1970s; it has been evolving ever since. A team of hardware and software engineers designed the OpenVMS operating system and the VAX computer so that the two complement one another. OpenVMS has been a supported product for 22 years. OpenVMS is not a "legacy" product but is actively supported by Hewlett-Packard Corporation (HP). OpenVMS 7.3-1 was released midway through the preparation of this manuscript. Nonetheless, commands and examples are based on OpenVMS 7.3. HP will even support selected versions of OpenVMS dating back to 1992 (5.5-2). User software developed for older versions of OpenVMS will often run without changes on newer versions. To get a feel for how many versions (currently about 35) have been released, look at riogrande.digital.com.au/pub/ecoinfo/ecoinfo/version.htm. Not all versions are supported by HP, however. OpenVMS 5.5-2, 6.2, and 7.2-2 (and later) are the only versions that a support contract with HP can be written against. Digging a bit deeper in this site will show how online downloads of corrections (patches) are supported.

OpenVMS supports multiprocessing and clustering of 96 systems spanning up to 100 kilometers. Version 7.3 was released in early 2001, but HP continues to support older versions either actively (through support contracts) or passively through downloadable patches (see, for instance, ftp://ftp.service.digital.com/public/vms/axp) and freeware (www.openvms.compaq.com/openvms/freeware

/freeware.html). There are also informal user groups, such as www.levitte.org/~ava/ and www.hobbesthevax.com/noframe.html, and a news group (comp.os.vms) that many experts, including HP employees, visit regularly. A hobbyist organization is sanctioned by HP as well. See www.montagar.com/hobbyist/index.html for details about the free hobby program.

A Brief History of Digital, Compaq, and Hewlett-Packard

Digital Equipment Corporation (DEC) was founded by Ken Olsen in 1957. In those days the word *computer* conjured up visions of mammoth machines in huge rooms with one glass wall for visitor viewing. This is not the future Olsen saw, and hence he did not want that word in his company title. Instead, Olsen's view for computers was a ubiquitous laboratory instrument. Unfortunately, he never imagined his computers in the hands of individuals. In 1992 Olsen retired. In 1998 DEC was sold to Compaq in the largest-ever acquisition in the industry. Finally, in 2002, Compaq was sold to Hewlett-Packard.

Compaq was founded by three Texas Instruments (TI) dropouts—Rod Canion, Jim Harris, and Bill Murto—in 1982. By 1987 Compaq had built 1 million computers. Compaq has never been an engineering company in the sense that DEC was and HP is today; however, Compaq was innovative in that it was the first company to even attempt to beat IBM at its own game in the PC market. IBM's PC was taking corporate America by storm, and no one could touch them because their software-hardware interface (called BIOS) was copyrighted and IBM was not licensing it to anyone. Compaq's founders reverse-engineered IBM's BIOS (a legal move to outwit the copyright protection) and produced the first IBM clone. This meant that any software written for an IBM PC would also run on a Compaq PC. From that point on IBM gradually lost the PC business, because Compaq and other clone makers could produce their products faster and cheaper than IBM. IBM's corporate mindset was still in mainframes and simply could not compete with the agile startups. IBM's reputation made the PC respectable for businesses, but Compaq's pricing and marketing made the PC more available and affordable. Of the three founders, only Canion spent significant time with the company. He moved out around 1991.

Hewlett-Packard began its corporate life in 1939 designing and manufacturing scientific instruments. Bill Hewlett and Dave Packard's first product (in 1938) was an audio signal generator used in Walt Disney's original version of *Fantasia*. In 1966 HP made its initial entry into the computer industry with the HP 2116A used to control test and measurement instruments. In 1968 HP introduced the desktop scientific calculator, the HP 9100A. It was advertised as a *personal computer*, the first time that term was used. In 1972 HP introduced the first scientific handheld calculator, the HP-35, banishing the slide rule forever.

In 1983 HP released its first versions of the PC called the HP-150. I bought my first computer in 1984—an HP-150. It was unique in two ways: (1) it had a finger-activated cursor (HP called it a touch screen), and (2) it had a 3 1/2-inch floppy drive.[1] HP's machine was incompatible with software written for IBM PCs, however, because of its incompatible BIOS, as described previously. Along with my HP-150, I also bought an HP ThinkJet printer, which was first available in 1984. It was a forerunner of most of today's inexpensive printers. Another long-forgotten HP innovation was the first truly portable PC, called the HP-110. It weighed only 8 pounds and had several built-in applications in ROM (this was before hard drives) and LCD display. It was clearly well ahead of its time, but it too was incompatible with IBM hardware and software. In 1986 HP was experimenting with RISC architecture. In 1994 HP began collaborating with Intel to develop what we now know as the IA-64, the Itanium.

Although HP computers never made much of a dent in the marketplace, its printers more than compensated for this deficiency. The laser printer was introduced in 1980, but that technology did not take off until the LaserJet (a spinoff on the ThinkJet) was introduced in 1984. That printer started the "laser printer wars" that are still going on today.

In 2000 HP's scientific instrument business was split off into a new company called Agilent Technologies, and the computer and printer business retained the HP name. Hewlett retired in 1987 and Packard retired in 1993. The garage in which Dave and Bill started the business in 1938 is now a California Registered Landmark.

A Brief History of Digital Hardware

When it began in 1957, DEC's engineers built logic modules, such as simple AND and OR gates, but by 1959, the engineers realized that these modules could become the basis of a computer. That is when the company built its first computer and called it the PDP-1. PDP is an acronym for programmable data processor; the word *computer* was still missing from DEC's terminology. In that era, fundamental computer architecture was still fluid, and DEC engineers were experimenting to find the optimum configuration. At that time the best combination of word size, register configuration, and instruction set had yet to be determined. Furthermore, the silicon technology was changing rapidly. The PDP-1, -4, -7, -9, and -15 were 18-bit machines; the PDP-5, -8, and -15 were 12-bit machines; and the PDP-6 and -10 were 36-bit machines. In many cases, these machines were being developed in parallel. The engineers did not achieve the best blend of features until the PDP-11, a 16-bit complex instruction set computer (CISC), which was released in 1970. DEC built more than 600,000 PDP-11s in various forms over the next 20 years. That machine is still manufactured and sold today, but not by Compaq/HP; it is licensed to Mentec.

---

1. Apple also introduced the 3 1/2-inch floppy with the first Macintosh in 1984.

By the mid-1970s, even though the PDP-11 was a tremendous success, DEC engineers recognized that its address space was too small, only 128K bytes, to keep up with software demands. In 1978 the VAX (Virtual Address eXtension to the PDP-11) was released. The VAX is a 32-bit CISC with more than 300 instructions. This machine was another hit for Olsen and DEC.

Once again, in 1993, the small computer was rocked by the AXP (not an acronym, just three letters) developed by DEC. This is a 64-bit RISC, an architecture deemed necessary because the industry had outgrown the VAX, just as it outgrew the PDP-11. The engineers believed the VAX had too little growth potential in CPU speed and address space. The AXP was later renamed the Alpha.

DEC was in decline, however. The introduction of the Alpha was far behind Sun's SPARC (a 32-bit RISC) designed in 1985 and HP's RISC work as well. In the late 1980s, the SPARC had effectively replaced DEC in the engineering workstation market. Even though Sun's 64-bit RISC was introduced about the same time as the Alpha, Sun's customer base remained loyal. DEC defined the "small"[1] computer industry (i.e., small compared with IBM's 360 mainframe series). DEC led that industry until the late 1980s.

A Brief History of Digital Software

OpenVMS was designed from the outset to be a secure, multiuser system with full networking functionality. In fact, the VAX and VMS were designed concurrently at DEC by a hardware/software engineering team. The VAX is a CISC and included many instructions designed expressly to support VMS. The Alpha is a reduced instruction set computer (RISC). As OpenVMS evolved, new features such as symmetric multiprocessing (SMP) and clustering were added.

The conversion of the PDP-11 customer base to the VAX was accomplished by moving much of the PDP-11 operating system, RSX-11, to the VAX. RSX could be invoked as a DCL command, and the VAX hardware was designed to execute the PDP-11 instruction set. Even so, the new operating system, VAX/VMS, was part of the VAX-11[2] release. Many OpenVMS concepts find their roots in RSX-11 (e.g., user identification code [UIC]; the name of the root directory, [000000]; and process privileges, to name a few). The DEC proprietary networking protocol, DECnet, is still compatible between a PDP-11/RSX-11 computer and an Alpha/OpenVMS computer.

Since 1993, OpenVMS has also been running on the 64-bit Alpha platform, a CPU pioneered by DEC and today, the primary OpenVMS host. About 50 Alpha models are

---

1. Digital engineers first coined the term minicomputer for the PDP-8 to describe their product line. The PDP-8 was the first computer to be priced at less than $10,000.
2. The VAX-11 name was a marketing ploy to entice loyal PDP-11 customers—to assure them that this new machine was not a significant departure from the PDP-11.

supported, although many are no longer manufactured. Unlike the PDP-11-to-VAX transition, the operating system was unchanged when the Alpha was introduced. To expedite the switchover, a conversion routine was written so that any VAX executable could be converted to run on the Alpha. This was not a sales gimmick; it was a powerful tool used by DEC software engineers to transfer much of the VAX software to the Alpha.

Even while Compaq and HP were discussing their merger, plans were made to port OpenVMS to the Itanium. OpenVMS on the Itanium (IA-64) is due to be released in 2003 and 2004 in several stages. The Itanium computer is HP/Intel's entry into the 64-bit world.

The VAX is no longer made, but OpenVMS for that platform is still supported on several dozen models (depending on how they are counted) of the VAX computer.

For the record, VMS and OpenVMS are two names for the same operating system. Originally, the operating system was called VAX-11/VMS; it changed to VAX/VMS at Version 2.0. When the VMS operating system was ported to the Alpha platform, it was renamed OpenVMS, for both VAX and Alpha computers. In part, this name change signified the high degree of support for industry standards such as POSIX, which provides many features found in UNIX systems. What became confusing was that the OpenVMS name was introduced first for OpenVMS AXP V1.0, causing the widespread misunderstanding that OpenVMS was for Alpha AXP only, whereas "regular VMS" was for VAX. In fact, the official name of the VAX operating system was changed as of V5.5, although the name was not used until V6.0 was released. The proper names for OpenVMS on the two platforms are now "OpenVMS VAX" and "OpenVMS Alpha," the latter having superseded "OpenVMS AXP."

As new hardware—both peripherals and CPUs—become available, OpenVMS is upgraded and re-released. Software bugs and improvements are also included in the upgrades. In order to define which hardware is supported by which version of OpenVMS, the software product description (SPD) is updated with each upgrade. The SPD also includes a list and brief description of software products that are licensed by HP. Some third-party software is listed in the document.

The operating system is designed to perform well under any SPD-defined environment and can simultaneously support processes that exhibit extensive I/O demands, those that exhibit extensive CPU demands, real-time processes, and client/server applications. OpenVMS automatically adapts itself to the number of CPUs, the amount of physical memory, and the number and type of disks attached to the computer.

There is a precise definition of the instruction set required for OpenVMS. The VAX supported "native" OpenVMS on most models. The instructions that were not built in were simulated in software; however, the base architecture of a given Alpha computer does not match this definition, so firmware (called PALcode) is loaded to emulate certain required OpenVMS instructions. System reference manual (SRM) console firmware controls the console before booting OpenVMS, and it is the boot program. It scans for the hardware configuration and stashes that information in memory for OpenVMS to access later. It initializes the CPU, cache control, memory management, and the basic I/O devices. Finally, it loads the primary boot program (the primary loads the secondary) from the system disk and transfers control to it.

A partial version of OpenVMS is available for the 86xx family. Called Charon-VAX, a product of Software Resources International (SRI), this effort is entirely independent of HP. It is available both commercially and for hobbyists. The URL is www.softresint.com/softresint/legal.htm. Charon-VAX is actually a MicroVAX emulator running as an application on Windows NT. The emulator is purchased from SRI, and OpenVMS is purchased from HP. Used VAX and Alpha computers can be purchased on eBay auction (search for VAX or DEC) and from any of several used computer companies.

OpenVMS Tutorial

The remainder of this chapter is an OpenVMS tutorial. It is brief and includes references for the reader who is interested in more details. This is information about OpenVMS that a manager, but not necessarily the unprivileged user, must know. Therefore, this section supplements the introductory topics found in most OpenVMS tutorials. Documents referenced in this section can be found at www.openvms.com:8000.

As with any other operating system, certain terms and concepts are unique to OpenVMS. The rest of this chapter introduces some of those unique characteristics. Without some understanding of Digital Command Language (DCL), the remainder of the book may not be as helpful as intended. This is by no means a complete treatment of the subject, however, and the reader is encouraged to delve into one of the references, especially Digital Press's *OpenVMS User's Guide,* before attempting any hands-on system management.

DCL is a command-line interface (not graphical) to the operating system. It tends to be more DOS-like than UNIX-like in that the commands are closer to English (e.g., dir, not ls). Commands (and file names) are not case sensitive, and most commands can be abbreviated.

Commands

DCL commands (sometimes called *verbs*) are the human-machine interface, like a UNIX shell. There is only one OpenVMS "shell" language. Commands are entered either interactively, from a command file (command program file or script[1]), or via a batch job (see Chapter 4). Commands are not case sensitive, but I will show them as uppercase to more easily distinguish them in the text. As a convenience, a freeware program called DCLCOMPLETE is available for OpenVMS on VAX computers. The user need only type the first few letters of the command and then press the <TAB> key. DCLCOMPLETE will echo the complete command on the screen. Likewise, DCLCOMPLETE will finish file names.

There is no concept in OpenVMS like the UNIX hash table. Instead, two mechanisms are used for command execution:

- Commands are defined in SYS$LIBRARY:DCLTABLES.EXE, which includes the complete syntactical definition of the command and the exact location of the executable image.

- To speed up access to commonly used images, they are declared to the system via the INSTALL command. This mechanism is also exploited to secure the system. This is somewhat like the combination of the UNIX sudo command and UID execution permission concept. See Chapter 8.

The system manager may extend DCLTABLES.EXE with SET COMMAND. A freeware utility called VERB can be used to display the contents of DCLTABLES.EXE. To give a flavor for the complexity of this data, a partial display of the DIRECTORY command is as follows:

```
$ VERB DIRECTORY

define verb DIRECTORY
    image DIRECTORY
    parameter P1, label=INPUT, prompt="File"
        value (list,impcat,type=$infile)
    qualifier ACL
    qualifier BACKUP
    qualifier BEFORE
        value (default="TODAY",type=$datetime)
    qualifier BRIEF, nonnegatable, default
    qualifier BY_OWNER
        value (type=$uic)
    qualifier COLUMNS, default
        value (default="4")
```

---

1. Command files offer additional capabilities unavailable to interactive entry, such as conditional execution and subroutines.

The HELP command (similar to the UNIX man) describes all of the commands. HELP HINTS is probably the best starting point for a novice user; however, HELP is intended only as an online reference. Here is an example of what HELP HINTS provides:

```
$ help hints

HINTS

   Type the name of one of the categories listed below to obtain a list
of related commands and topics.  To obtain detailed information on a
topic, press the RETURN key until you reach the "Topic?" prompt and
then type the name of the topic.

Additional information available:

   Batch_and_print_jobs  Command_procedures     Contacting_people
   Creating_processes    Developing_programs    Executing_programs
   Files_and_directories Logical_names          Operators_in_expressions
   Physical_devices      Security               System_management
   Terminal_environment  User_environment

HINTS Subtopic? command
```

The complete description for each command is given in the *OpenVMS DCL Dictionary* and in Chapter 3 of the *OpenVMS User's Manual*. Commands are English words that indicate the action to be taken (e.g., DIRECTORY, PRINT, and SEARCH) and can be abbreviated, in these cases to DIR, PRI, and SEA. DCL command syntax normally appears as follows:

```
$ verb [subverb] [[[/qualifier]=value]…] [[parameter]…]
```

where […] indicate optional fields.

Subverbs further limit the verb (e.g., SET and SHOW have many subverbs). In order to display the current date and time, use the following command. In this example, TIME is a subverb and the space is required:

```
$ SHOW TIME
```

Command qualifiers (sometimes called *switches*) modify the action of the verb. Qualifiers are English words such as LIST and OUTPUT. Qualifiers are consistent across all commands. For instance, if the maximum detail is to be displayed for a command, the qualifier /FULL is always used rather than a confusing variation in which some commands use /FULL and others use /ALL. Qualifiers may be abbreviated also.

The following command displays detailed information about the previous command's error message. Notice that there is no subverb and no parameter. The space is optional.

```
$ HELP /MESSAGE
```

The previous command is particularly helpful to a novice. It provides useful information about a particular error message. For instance, falling back on UNIX habits, I might enter:

```
$ Man show
%DCL-IVVERB, unrecognized command verb - check validity and
spelling
 \MAN\
```

Because OpenVMS error messages may be unfamiliar, a better explanation might be required. Using the HELP/MESS in the following example, OpenVMS displays additional detailed information. Notice also that this example illustrates that OpenVMS is not case sensitive.

```
$ help/mess ivverb

IVVERB,  unrecognized command verb - check validity and spelling

   Facility:     CLI, Command Language Interpreter (DCL)

   Explanation:  The first word in the command is not a valid DCL
                 command or a symbol name equated with a command.
                 The rejected portion of the command is displayed
                 between backslashes.

   User Action:  Check the spelling of the command name or symbol
                 name, then reenter the command.
```

Some qualifiers require values. Some verbs require parameters, usually in the form of file names. This final example shows a command with all of the fields present. Also notice that the command has multiple qualifiers. It will print pages 3 through 6 of the specified file and display the file's name on the top of each page.

```
$ PRINT /HEADER/PAGE=(3:6) MYFILE.TXT
```

Editing a command is done with a combination of the left- and right-arrow keys and the delete/backspace key. Control-A toggles between overwrite and insert mode for the corrections. The up- and down-arrow keys can be used to scroll through previously entered command lines. The RECALL command can be used to display a full screen of previously entered commands, or it can be used to search for a specific command.

For the benefit of the system manager and users, several HELP files are available in the SYS$HELP directory. The following command lists the latest version of all help libraries (.HLB;0):

```
$ DIR SYS$HELP:*.HLB;0
Directory SYS$COMMON:[SYSHLP]

ACLEDT.HLB;1          ACS$DWCI.HLB;3        ADA$DWCI.HLB;3
ANALAUDIT$HELP.HLB;1                        ANLRMSHLP.HLB;1       ATK$HELP.HLB;6
BKM$HELP.HLB;1        CC$DWCI.HLB;2         CLUE.HLB;1            CMS$DW_HELP.HLB;1
DBG$DSHELP.HLB;1      DBG$DSUIHELP.HLB;1    DBG$HELP.HLB;1        DBG$UIHELP.HLB;1
DECCHART$MOTIF.HLB;1                        DECSET$ENVMGR.HLB;3
DECW$DXMHELP_HELP.HLB;1                     DECW$HELPHELP.HLB;1 DECW$MAIL.HLB;1
DECW$PRINTWGT.HLB;1 DEFRAGMENT.HLB;1        DISKQUOTA.HLB;1       DTEHELP.HLB;1
DTRHELP.HLB;1        DTSDTR.HLB;1           EDFHLP.HLB;1          EDTHELP.HLB;1
ESS$LADCP.HLB;1      ESS$LASTCPHELP.HLB;1                         EVE$HELP.HLB;1
EVE$KEYHELP.HLB;1    EXCHNGHLP.HLB;1        FORTRAN$DWCI.HLB;2    FTP.HLB;1
HELPLIB.HLB;13       INSTALHLP.HLB;1        IPNCP.HLB;1           KERMIT.HLB;1
LANCP$HELP.HLB;1     LAST.HLB;1             LATCP$HELP.HLB;1      LMCP$HLB.HLB;1
LSE$CLIHELP.HLB;2    LSE$HELP.HLB;2         LSE$KEYPAD.HLB;3      LSE$MENU.HLB;3
LSEHELP.HLB;1        LWK$LBASE_HELP.HLB;2                         MACRO$DWCI.HLB;1
MAILHELP.HLB;1       MAILUAF.HLB;1          MMG.HLB;1             MMS$DW_HELP.HLB;1
MNRHELP.HLB;1        MSA$MANAGER.HLB;6      NCPHELP.HLB;1         NOTES$DWHELP.HLB;2
NOTES$HELP.HLB;2     PASCAL$DWCI.HLB;2      PATCHHELP.HLB;1       PCDISKHLP.HLB;12
PCSA_MANAGER.HLB;7   PHONEHELP.HLB;1        PRETTY.HLB;1          PSDC$EDITHELP.HLB;1
PSDC$FILES.HLB;1     PSPA$COMMAND.HLB;1     PWRK$ADMIN.HLB;5
PWRK$MOP_MANAGER.HLB;5                      PWRK$PCSA_MANAGER.HLB;5
PWRK$SHOWINI.HLB;5   PWRK$UPGRADE.HLB;5     SDA.HLB;1             SHWCLHELP.HLB;1
SSU$HELP.HLB;1       SYSGEN.HLB;1           SYSMANHELP.HLB;1      TECO.HLB;1
TELNET.HLB;1         TFF$TFUHELP.HLB;1      TPUHELP.HLB;1         UAFHELP.HLB;1
UCX$FTP_HELP.HLB;7   UCX$NSLOOKUP_HELP.HLB;4
UCX$TELNET_HELP.HLB;7                       UCX$UCP_HELP.HLB;7    UISHELP.HLB;1
VAXAPL.HLB;1         VUIT.HLB;2             WCP_HELPLIB.HLB;1     WP.HLB;1
WRITE$EQUATION.HLB;1                        WRITE$HELP.HLB;1      XMODEM.HLB;1

Total of 94 files.
```

Normally, these help libraries are accessed by the particular utility through its internal HELP command. For instance, the following command accesses UAFHELP.HLB:

```
$ run authorize
UAF> help

  Information available:

   ADD        Command_Summary     COPY      CREATE     DEFAULT     EXIT
   GRANT      HELP      LIST       MODIFY    REMOVE     RENAME      REVOKE
   SHOW       Usage_Summary

Topic?
```

Files and Devices

OpenVMS file names are more like the DOS / Windows standard than the UNIX standard. There are actually two file structures supported by OpenVMS, called ODS-2^1 and ODS-5. The latter is Windows NT and UNIX style naming: upper- and lowercase, blanks, and other special characters are permitted. ODS-2 is more restrictive: no special characters (with some exceptions) and case insensitive. A fully qualified ODS-2 file name has the following format:

```
node::device:[directory.sub-dir.sub-sub-dir]file.extension;version
```

The punctuation (::, :, [,], ., and ;) is important, and spaces are not permitted in any part of the file name. Reading from the left, node refers to the network name of the computer. See Chapter 9 for the network discussion. OpenVMS files are based on devices, not partitions like most other operating systems. Devices are made known to OpenVMS via the MOUNT command. Each disk is rooted at a directory called [000000],[1] and there is only one root on a device. There are no tools that search for a particular file across multiple devices.

The file name and extension are limited to 39 characters, although certain three-letter extensions have special meanings and conventions in OpenVMS, much like DOS's conventions. Some examples are presented as follows:

- COM is a command procedure file.

- CC is a C source file.

- CXX is a C++ source file.

- DIR is a directory file. The UNIX convention, . and .., is not used in OpenVMS.

- EXE is an executable file created by LINK.

- LIS is a displayable or printable file usually created by a compiler.

- OBJ is an object file created by a complier.

Unlike any other operating system, the existence of multiple copies of a file is supported by OpenVMS. Usually this is an automatic feature supported by the editors, and DCL commands such as COPY also create a new version. A limit to the number of versions can be managed at either the file level or at any level in the directory tree. Usually the system manager sets up the user directory tree to limit five versions of all files. Thus, when the sixth version is created, the oldest file (based on version number) with the same name is deleted. The version number is suffixed to the file name and separated from the file name with a semicolon. File concepts are discussed in the *OpenVMS User's Manual*, Chapters 4 and 5.

---

1. ODS-1 is the file system used on PDP-11 (hardware) running RSX (an operating system called a Resource Sharing Executive). RSX is the immediate ancestor of OpenVMS. Early versions of VMS (not OpenVMS) supported ODS-1 so that RSX applications and users could easily migrate to VMS. ODS means On-Disk Structure.
1. [000000] was chosen for historical reasons. [000,000] was the root of the ODS-1 file system.

An example of a DIRECTORY command, as follows, illustrates how the fully qualified file name is presented to the user. The node name is not displayed, but all versions are shown. To display additional information about the files, additional qualifiers are added to the DIRECTORY command:

```
$ dir login
Directory FACULTY:[DMILLER]
LOGIN.COM;101        LOGIN.COM;100        LOGIN.COM;99
```

ODS-5 files were added to OpenVMS with release 7.2, but this function is not fully implemented at this time. The complete description document is called *OpenVMS Guide to Extended File Specifications*. OpenVMS supports both conventions on a single system, but the user (and system manager) must be aware of certain restrictions that this feature imposes (e.g., how a file name with more than one dot is parsed). Furthermore, ODS-5 names are not fully supported by some layered products (e.g., many compilers) but are supported by others (e.g., Java).

OpenVMS will support RAID 0 and 5 (striping with or without parity) across a maximum of 32 disks, permitting very large directory trees. OpenVMS will also support a rooted file tree across several devices. This function is similar to striping, except each file resides on a single physical disk. This structure is called a Bound Volume Set. RAID 1 (mirroring) across a maximum of three disks is also permitted. See the *OpenVMS User's Manual*, Chapter 14, which discusses variations.

The OpenVMS file manager, Record Management System (RMS), supports three distinct file formats. All OpenVMS files should be thought of as record-oriented, not character-oriented as UNIX files are. The file formats are the following:

- *Sequential access* (somewhat like UNIX files except at the record level). To access the nth record, all n-1 records must be first read (or written). Going backward in the file is not permitted; instead, the file must be first repositioned at the beginning. This class is subdivided (e.g., FORTRAN-generated files are uniquely identified because the first character of the line is a printer carriage control).

- *Relative access*. All records in this class are the same length; thus, to read the nth record, RMS will skip n-1 records and directly access the desired record. Relative access files are bidirectional in that records can be accessed in any order. The file may be written in any order as well. Multiple users may read and write relative access files simultaneously.

- *Indexed access*. All records contain at least one "key" field. The records are accessed according to the key, not according to the record's position in the file. Hence, the file is randomly accessed using a key field in the data itself. This is a logical extension of relative access files in that the data (rather than a record number) is used to read and write records.

Several utilities are included in OpenVMS to create, manage, and optimize these files. In particular, indexed files must be defined (with CREATE/FDL) before they can be populated (using CONVERT) with data. To examine a file's characteristics, ANALYZE/RMS is used. The following display shows a portion of the information displayed by this command. Because of its complexity, the display for this file is four pages long, but only a portion is shown, as follows:

```
$ analyze/rms sys$system:sysuaf

Check RMS File Integrity                  14-SEP-2002 17:01:16.06
Page 1
SYS$COMMON:[SYSEXE]SYSUAF.DAT;1


FILE HEADER

        File Spec: SYS$COMMON:[SYSEXE]SYSUAF.DAT;1
        File ID: (9370,11,0)
        Owner UIC: [SYSTEM]
        Protection:  System: RWE, Owner: RWE, Group: RWE, World:
        Creation Date:   19-JUN-1998 11:34:34.67
        Revision Date:   14-SEP-2002 17:00:52.16, Number: 26183
        Expiration Date: none specified
        Backup Date:     none posted
        Contiguity Options:  contiguous-best-try
        Performance Options: none
        Reliability Options: none
        Journaling Enabled:  none


RMS FILE ATTRIBUTES

        File Organization: indexed
        Record Format: variable
        Record Attributes:
        Maximum Record Size: 1412
        Blocks Allocated: 670, Default Extend Size: 3
        Bucket Size: 3
        File Monitoring: disabled
        Global Buffer Count: 100
```

File characteristics are changed with the SET FILE command. Thus, the UNIX commands—chmod, chown, and chgrp—are all rolled into SET FILE. Because OpenVMS supports so many different file types, SET FILE has many more capabilities.

The file database is kept in the devices root directory, [000000]. The two most important files are BITMAP.SYS, containing the disk's bitmap, and INDEXF.SYS, which is a bitmap indicating the status of each file's descriptions (also called *file headers*).

There are no tools to examine BITMAP.SYS, but ANALYZE/DISK/REPAIR will correct it if necessary. INDEXF.SYS can be examined with DUMP:

```
$ DUMP/HEADER/BLOCK=COUNT=0 LOGIN.COM

Dump of file FACULTY:[DMILLER]LOGIN.COM;101 on 18-OCT-2002 15:06:26.47
File ID (23019,49,0)   End of file block 7 / Allocated 9

                            File Header

Header area
    Identification area offset:        40
    Map area offset:                   100
    Access control area offset:        249
    Reserved area offset:              255
    Extension segment number:          0
    Structure level and version:       2, 1
    File identification:               (23019,49,0)
    Extension file identification:     (0,0,0)
    VAX-11 RMS attributes
        Record type:                   Variable
        File organization:             Sequential
        Record attributes:             Implied carriage control
        Record size:                   75
        Highest block:                 9
        End of file block:             7
        End of file byte:              8
        Bucket size:                   0
        Fixed control area size:       0
        Maximum record size:           255
        Default extension size:        0
        Global buffer count:           0
        Directory version limit:       0
    File characteristics:              <none specified>
    Map area words in use:             2
    Access mode:                       0
    File owner UIC:                    [DMILLER]
    File protection:                   S:RWED, O:RWED, G:, W:
    Back link file identification:     (766,2,0)
    Journal control flags:             <none specified>
    Active recovery units:             None
    Highest block written:             7

Identification area
    File name:                         LOGIN.COM;101
    Revision number:                   8
    Creation date:                     24-MAR-1999 07:51:35.60
    Revision date:                     10-AUG-2002 12:05:26.23
    Expiration date:                   <none specified>
    Backup date:                       <none specified>
```

```
Map area
    Retrieval pointers
        Count:          9       LBN:    1937841

Access Control List
    (IDENTIFIER=DM_RIGHT,ACCESS=READ)

Checksum:                               16655
```

The DIRECTORY command is used to both list files and to find files in a directory tree. This single command combines the capabilities of the two UNIX commands: ls and find. To find a command within a directory tree, the ellipses (. . .) syntax is used. For example, to find DCLTABLES.EXE anywhere on the system disk, the system manager would use the command:

```
$ DIR SYS$SYSDISK:[000000...]DCLTABLES.EXE
```

Only SYSTEM has access to the root directory for security reasons.

Logical Definitions

Logical names are somewhat like environment variables in NT and UNIX. Usually, a logical name applies to file name. For instance, SYS$SYSTEM is the logical name of the directory in which many of the OpenVMS utilities reside. More generally, OpenVMS products reside in their own directory (e.g., the HELP facility files are located in the SYS$HELP directory). Systemwide logicals are defined at boot time in SYLOGICALS.COM; however, local logicals are defined when a user logs in (e.g., SYS$LOGIN is the user's directory and SYS$INPUT is the user's terminal). In the following example, FACULTY is a logical and not to be confused with [FACULTY.] the subdirectory. The SHOW command displays its definition. In English, this display indicates that the FACULTY logical is equated with (or synonymous to) the BEAVER$DKB0 disk drive and rooted at [000000.FACULTY]. In this definition, the dot is included to make it easier to use.

```
$ show logical faculty
    "FACULTY" = "BEAVER$DKB0:[FACULTY.]" (LNM$SYSTEM_TABLE)
```

The device name in the previous definition is coded this way: BEAVER is the name of the node to which the disk is physically attached, and the $ is a lexical separator. The DK means it is a SCSI device; B stands for the second device channel installed in the computer; and 0 is the SCSI address. The DCL tool used to create logicals is DEFINE. Logicals are discussed in some detail in Chapter 32 of the *OpenVMS Programming Concepts Manual*.

If [DMILLER] is a subdirectory of [FACULTY.] (the [000000.] is unnecessary), then the following command permits an authorized user to list a file's characteristics. The benefit of this scheme is that the physical device name does not need to be known.

```
$ DIR FACULTY:[DMILLER]LOGIN.COM
```

Although logicals usually are equated to files, they are not restricted to that purpose. Logical definitions are stored in tables. In the previous example, the table name is displayed on the right in brackets. Each logical table has an access privilege associated with it. This prohibits the user from changing systemwide logicals such as SYS$SYSDISK, the logical name of the system disk. Logical definitions residing in system tables are retained until the system is shut down. Systemwide logical definitions, such as FACULTY, are normally placed in SYS$MANAGER:SYLOGICALS.COM by the manager. This specially named file is automatically executed by the boot script. The boot sequence is discussed in Chapter 2.

Any user may create his or her private logicals, which no other user may access. In fact, the user may create a private definition for SYS$SYSDISK, although that is probably a bad idea. Personal logical definitions are automatically destroyed at the end of the session.

Symbols

Symbols are created with the assignment operation. Most often they are defined in command procedures. The manager usually includes assignment statements and logical definitions in SYS$MANAGER:SYLOGIN.COM, thus making them universal for all users because SYLOGIN.COM is a script invoked before the user's LOGIN.COM file. Used in this way, a symbol is like a UNIX alias. Assignment is discussed in the *OpenVMS DCL Dictionary* in the Assignment Statement and String Assignment sections.

LOGIN.COM is commonly found in all user accounts and is the equivalent of UNIX's .login. It is a command procedure (or script file) that is invoked automatically each time a user logs in. Symbols created in LOGIN.COM are private and inaccessible by other users. A typical user assignment is shown as follows. It creates a new symbol, LS (which, after it is defined, can be used like a verb), to customize the DIRECTORY command:

```
$ LS :== DIR/SIZE/COL=1
```

When entered by the user, it would produce the following display:

```
$ ls login.com

Directory FACULTY:[DMILLER]
```

```
LOGIN.COM;101                    7
LOGIN.COM;100                    7
LOGIN.COM;99                     7

Total of 3 files, 21 blocks.
```

Incidentally, in OpenVMS, file sizes are measured in units of blocks, not characters. A *block* is 512 characters.

Logicals and symbols are often confused. In simplistic terms, there are two differences:

1. *Logicals are recursive, but symbols are not.* That is, a logical may be defined using another logical, but a symbol defined in this way cannot contain another symbol.

2. *Logicals are translated anywhere in the command line, but symbols are translated only at the left side of the command.* This means DIR SYSUAF and LS are the proper usage for the definitions. DIR LS would result in an error message.

Symbols are also used in command procedures as computational variables in the traditional, computer language sense. For instance:

```
$ counter = counter + 1
```

and

```
$ spaces = columna + width*5
```

There are other, more subtle differences between logicals and symbols. The definitive resources are Digital Press's *Writing Real Programs in DCL*, Chapter 14, and the *OpenVMS User's Manual*, Chapters 14, 15, and 16.

Life of a Process

Unlike UNIX, piping and child processes are not part of the OpenVMS paradigm, although both facilities are available. When a user logs in, a process is created. As DCL commands are entered, they are executed in the context of that same process; no child is created. Likewise, there are no background processes as in UNIX. Instead, the user creates subprocesses with the SPAWN/NOWAIT command. Alternately, command procedures can be queued to a batch queue using the SUBMIT command, although this facility is normally used only for executing a lengthy series of commands. Batch jobs are not interactive.

OpenVMS executes one *image* (also called *executable file*) after another in the context of the login process. This is unlike UNIX, which creates a child process for each command. In OpenVMS, normally only one process is created from login to logout. Creation of a process is a relatively expensive operation (in terms of CPU time and file accesses), whereas activation of an image is inexpensive. Processes are discussed in detail in Chapter 18 of the *OpenVMS User's Manual*.

From a user's viewpoint, all of the system images he or she needs are ready to execute. For instance, commands to invoke compilers and editors are defined. But from the system manager's viewpoint, not all system tools are defined to execute so easily. In particular, many of the tools in SYS$SYSTEM must be executed in one of two ways (the two are equivalent):

- By prefixing the file name with RUN, for instance RUN SYS$SYSTEM:AUTHORIZE (no file name abbreviations are permitted).

- By prefixing the file name with MCR,[1] for instance MCR AUTHORIZE (again, no abbreviations are permitted). In this case OpenVMS assumes the image is in SYS$SYSTEM.

The more convenient method, however, is to define a symbol (discussed previously) in the SYSTEM account's LOGIN.COM by adding a line similar to this one:

```
$ UAF :== RUN SYS$SYSTEM:AUTHORIZE
```

or the shorthand form

```
$ UAF :== $SYS$SYSTEM:AUTHORIZE[2]
```

This assignment creates a "new" verb, UAF, and permits the system manager to simply enter UAF at the prompt to invoke the AUTHORIZE.EXE utility. The leading $-sign implies the verb RUN. In order to avoid confusion, however, this book does not take the liberty of assuming that any of these shortcuts exist.

Each process (and subprocess) has many quota limits, which OpenVMS manages. Even the SYSTEM account is subject to these quotas. These are shown with the SHOW PROCESS/QUOTA command in the following example:

```
$ show process/quota
17-AUG-2002 18:30:53.71   User: DMILLER      Process ID:    202060A4
                          Node: BEAVER       Process name:  "DMILLER"
```

---

1. MCR is a term that dates to the RSX operating system. The acronym stands for Monitor Console Routine, which is the "shell" of RSX. It was carried into the early VMS world to permit easy migration from RSX.
2. This $ prefix convention also dates to RSX usage, where system executables were stored in the [3,54] directory.

```
Process Quotas:
 Account name:
 CPU limit:                          Infinite  Direct I/O limit:          100
   Buffered I/O byte count quota:      49872  Buffered I/O limit:        100
   Timer queue entry quota:               10  Open file quota:           100
   Paging file quota:                  48453  Subprocess quota:            8
   Default page fault cluster:            64  AST quota:                 198
   Enqueue quota:                       4000  Shared file limit:           0
   Max detached processes:                 0  Max active jobs:            10
```

Only a few of these quotas will be described. The "Paging file quota" defines the size limit of the process (i.e., a process cannot grow in memory indefinitely). The "Subprocess quota" defines the limit of child processes that can be active simultaneously. "Max active jobs" limits the number of simultaneous logins.

OpenVMS not only regulates quota limits, but it also records actual resources usage for accounting and performance purposes. A typical display follows:

```
$ show process/accounting
Accounting information:
  Buffered I/O count:        150  Peak working set size:       458
  Direct I/O count:           30  Peak virtual size:          4451
  Page faults:              1673  Mounted volumes:               0
  Images activated:           14
  Elapsed CPU time:          0 00:00:00.54
  Connect time:              0 00:01:06.84
```

This information can be useful to charge the user for resources consumed. If a user exceeds any of the quota limits, this information is helpful in determining which one is causing the problem. The point is that resources for every account are restricted, managed, and measured. The out-of-the-box user default configuration is adequate for a "normal" account; however, the manager may need to increase these quotas via RUN AUTHORIZE for special cases. For instance, the quotas may have to be adjusted for Motif users. User account management is discussed more fully in Chapter 4. Accounting is discussed in Chapter 7.

As an image executes, two important attributes are modified. The first managed attribute is CPU time. The process's[1] priority is increased if it tends to be interactive and decreased if it tends to be CPU-bound. This means that CPU-bound processes are executed only if there are no interactive processes ready for execution. Furthermore, when an interactive process needs to run, the CPU process is suspended. This is called *preemptive scheduling*. This dynamic priority scheme is enforced by OpenVMS in order to favor keyboard response time, thus making the system as interactive as possible.

The second attribute that is carefully managed by OpenVMS is physical memory. Pages of an image are copied from disk to physical memory as needed. This activity is

---

1. Technically the executing image is one component of the process. The process includes the image, the DCL shell, and the OpenVMS kernel.

termed *demand paging*. Every process has a limited physical memory quota, however, and at some point, when a new page is requested, it must replace an old one belonging to the process. The old one is either written in the "page file" (if it has been modified) or discarded (if there are no changes on the page.) If all of physical memory is consumed, inactive processes are copied to the "swap file." Then the physical memory quota of all active processes is reduced to accommodate additional processes.

Privileged Images

Privileged images are a major security mechanism used by OpenVMS. This is the way OpenVMS allows an unprivileged user to perform operations he or she is not normally permitted to do. For instance, the commands SHOW USER (the UNIX equivalent of who) and SHOW SYSTEM (the UNIX equivalent of ps) must access normally inaccessible databases to extract information that is to be displayed. When a user executes a privileged image, it is executed in the context of the login process. This is done by granting additional privileges to the user's process temporarily, executing that image, and finally removing those privileges again. Normally, images are installed with privileges at boot time using the INSTALL command. It is the responsibility of OpenVMS to locate the privileged image in the installed database, modify user privileges, and execute the image. Any abnormal termination of a privileged image also removes the special privileges from the user process to maintain system security. Naturally, INSTALL is a privileged command that only the manager can use. This concept is expanded in Chapter 8.

Superuser

To become a "superuser" in OpenVMS, you must log into the system account (or some other account you created with all privileges). Alternatively, log in to any account, and enter the command

```
$ SET HOST 0   ! read set host zero
```

which will allow anyone to log in again. This is a more general form of the su command in UNIX. When logged into SYSTEM, the manager should be in the root of the SYS$MANAGER directory tree.

In the name of security, the OpenVMS out-of-the-box SYSTEM account's password expires every 30 days, whereas user passwords expire after 90 days. When installing OpenVMS for the first time, the manager must supply a password for SYSTEM; there is no default password option.

Related Publications

1. The OpenVMS novice is encouraged to read Digital Press's *OpenVMS User's Guide*, second edition, by Patrick Holmay. If you've never used OpenVMS before, this is the best introduction available to OpenVMS's basic commands, editors, the file structure, and an introduction to command procedures (i.e., script writing).

2. A second OpenVMS novice book also published by Digital Press (but originally imprinted as CBM Books) is called *Introduction to OpenVMS*, fourth edition, by Lesley Ogilvie. This book is a more cursory treatment of OpenVMS than the *User's Guide,* but it covers more territory.

3. Although it is a bit dated now, *OpenVMS Software Overview* is a good introductory document that defines many of the OpenVMS capabilities and features.

4. The Software Product Description (SPD) for OpenVMS 7.3 is called *Compaq OpenVMS Operating System for Alpha and VAX, Version 7.3.*

5. The OpenVMS online HELP facility is easy to use and a complete reference.

6. I've found the best starting point to reach the user community is www.levitte.org/~ava/. This site seems to point to everything else available, including DEC/Compaq/HP sites.

7. The official FAQ is www.openvms.compaq.com/wizard/openvms_faq.html. This information is actively updated regularly; however, this isn't the only FAQ available. See www.levitte.org/~ava/vms_faq.htmlx for others.

8. The command language bible is *Writing Real Programs in DCL* by Anagnostopoulos and Hoffman. This is required reading for system managers.

9. Hewlett-Packard maintains OpenVMS training for system managers online at www.openvms.compaq.com/training.html.

10. Ken Olsen's biography, and Digital's too of course, is recorded in *The Ultimate Entrepreneur: The Story of Ken Olsen and Digital Equipment Corporation* by Rifkin and Harrar. It was published in 1988, so it's not the whole story.

11. *Digital At Work: Snapshots from the First Thirty-Five Years*, edited by Jamie Pearson, is a composite of recollections and some great pictures. This book was published in 1992, so no Alpha stories are included.

12. *Computer Engineering: A DEC View of Hardware Systems Design*, by Bell, Mudge, and McNamara, contains the nitty-gritty of the hardware design constraints DEC engineers had to manage. Gordon Bell was DEC's chief hardware architect.

Although technologically dated, Bell's general observations probably still hold in computer design today.

13. *Guide to OpenVMS File Applications* describes OpenVMS files types and their applications.

Chapter 2 — Booting and Startup Script

OpenVMS has the capability to:

- Boot with minimal operator intervention.

- Boot in any of several unusual circumstances.

- Reconfigure itself for optimal site-specific operation.

- Dump memory before shutdown.

- Examine key operating system data structures while operating.

Normally, the hardware will start booting when power is applied, but this action can be configured to start with the console prompt instead. Furthermore, once at the console prompt, standard hardware tests can be performed one at a time, or various extended diagnostics can be performed on the hardware components. There are various types of boot options, which will be explained in detail:

- Default

- Conversational (to interactively adjust system parameters and enter SYSTEM password)

- Standalone (for certain disk backup and restore situations)

Boot Process

When the machine—either VAX or Alpha—is turned on, it performs a hardware test on memory and the installed controllers. Next, the hardware initialization program searches for attached peripherals. Finally, it displays the >>> prompt, called the "dead sergeant" to signal that the console program is ready.

There are several options available at the >>> prompt depending on the hardware model. Typically, more extensive hardware tests can be performed, disks can be initialized, and controllers can be configured. Most systems support a HELP command in some form to guide the manager; however, the operator's manual is essential for any extensive dialogs at this point. because each hardware model has unique capabilities and command syntax.

If the console program is configured to halt when powered up, the manager must enter a command to start the boot process. The command varies by hardware model, but usually a "B" will start the boot from a default device. The console program can be reconfigured to boot from a specific disk, instructed to continue without operator intervention into the OpenVMS boot procedure, and to permit remote boot commands.

On the VAX, the console program is in PROM and is not easily upgraded. On the Alpha, the System Reference Manual (SRM) console firmware controls the console before booting OpenVMS. This firmware is upgraded from time to time by Compaq/HP to reflect new hardware peripherals. The firmware can be downloaded from the Compaq site and upgraded by the manager. Whenever OpenVMS is installed or upgraded, the manager must check the firmware version number for compatibility.

VMB.EXE, the primary boot program, is located on the book disk; however, in early versions of the VAX, this program was either in ROM or a floppy disk. VMB's task is to locate the secondary boot program, SYS$SYSTEM:SYSBOOT.EXE, on disk, load it, and start it. Actually, VMB is a general-purpose boot program whose actions are determined by commands entered at the console. These other capabilities of VMB are beyond the intent of this book. Goldenberg discusses them in some detail (see the Bibliography).

Once SYSBOOT is running, it reads and saves SYS$SYSTEM:VAXVMSSYS.PAR on a VAX or ALPHAVMSSYS.PAR on an Alpha. This file contains all of the machine-specific parameters required to tune OpenVMS to the specific hardware and software configuration. Information in this file is used extensively throughout OpenVMS to control its performance. Then SYSBOOT locates and loads SYS$SYSTEM:EXE$INIT. The xVMSSYS.PAR file is managed automatically by a script called AUTOGEN or manually with the SYSMAN PARAMETER command.

Returning to the boot process, EXE$INIT initializes key data structures for process scheduling and memory management. Then it creates the first OpenVMS resident process called SWAPPER. When SWAPPER is started, it must initialize its local database to correspond with physical memory. The SWAPPER process controls memory management functions for OpenVMS and, therefore, runs continuously monitoring, and if necessary, adding or removing physical pages from each process. Once SWAPPER is running, the boot process has progressed to the point that OpenVMS is running as a time-sharing system, although it cannot yet support logins. SWAPPER also initializes several other OpenVMS kernel routines and databases. Finally, SWAPPER creates and starts a new process, SYSINIT, and then returns to its memory management duties.

SYSINIT loads the rest of the resident parts of OpenVMS and initializes cluster communications if the machine is a member of a cluster. It creates and starts another process, STARTUP, and exits. STARTUP is responsible for executing a machine-independent script called SYS$SYSTEM:STARTUP.COM. This script acts as the executive for all of the activity that will follow (i.e., for starting the OpenVMS support processes such as the file cache server, operator communications, audit server, job control, disk shadow server, license checking, and installation of layered products—e.g., compilers). This activity ends with the execution of two scripts, SYLOGICALS.COM and SYSTARTUP_VMS.COM, which are described in the next section.

Default Boot

Once the default boot command is entered, the standard boot procedure described previously begins. The STARTUP process is the host under which about 50 command files are executed in a specific order. Most of these files are not intended to be modified by the manager, but there are exceptions. The last two, SYLOGICALS and SYSSTARTUP_VMS, are intended to be customized by the manager to reflect the specific software installed on the system. SYS$MANAGER:SYLOGICALS defines systemwide logicals, and the manager may need to insert additions. SYS$MANAGER:SYSTARTUP_VMS[1] performs site-specific and possibly cluster node–specific operations. The system manager normally tailors this command procedure as well. Typical tasks performed by SYSTARTUP_VMS include (but are not limited to) the following:

- Mounting public disks

- Initializing and starting print and batch queues

- Installing privileged images

- Starting detached processes (called *daemons* in UNIX), also called *symbionts*

- Starting network protocols

- Housekeeping accounting and log files

- Defining systemwide announcements displayed at user login

SYSTARTUP_VMS will be referenced often in the chapters that follow. SYSTARTUP_VMS ends by defining the maximum number of interactive users supported by the system, thus activating interactive logins.

Conversational Boot

In certain exceptional cases, usually in emergencies, alternative boot procedures are also defined. These options modify the boot process described previously either by stopping part way through or by skipping through the process. The specific

1. Before OpenVMS Version 6, this file is called SYSTARTUP_Vx, where x is the version number.

alternative is indicated by adding parameters (or control flags) to the boot command. For example, on several Alpha models, a conversational boot is started with the command

```
>>> boot -flags 0,1 device_name
```

The user manual for each computer model specifies the specific syntax of this command. With this command, it is possible to stop the boot process in SYSBOOT (introduced earlier). Some reasons for a conversational boot are as follows:

- Loss of SYSTEM password

- Incorrect setting of a system parameter in xVMSSYS.PAR that prevents OpenVMS from starting because of limited resources

- Error in a startup script, notably SYSTARTUP_VMS, that prevents its completion

Once in SYSBOOT, several system utilities, particularly AUTHORIZE and SYSMAN, are available for use at the console, but only at the console, because OpenVMS has not yet started. When the required change is made, the manager has the option to either continue booting or stopping the boot and shutting down the system. If the manager wishes to continue booting, he or she has the following additional options:

- *Use the alternative SYSUAF.* If privileged account passwords are lost, the alternative SYSUAF can be substituted for the real one.

- *Minimal startup.* Continue the boot normally, but do not execute SYSTARTUP_VMS. This permits repair of SYSTARTUP_VMS.COM.

- *Bypass startup.* This option bypasses the execution of all startup scripts but starts a minimal system, which can be used to repair damaged script files.

- *Reverting to previous xVMSSYS.PAR file.* Occasionally, the manager may inadvertently or accidentally enter bad OpenVMS parameter data. If he or she does not immediately know what went wrong, the previously correct parameter file, xVMSSYS.OLD, can be used instead of the current one.

Details of the previous operations are not included in this book because of the intricacies involved. These details are provided in *OpenVMS System Management Guide*, Chapter 4, and the *System Manager's Manual*, Chapter 4.

Standalone Boot

A *standalone boot* is a term used when booting from a specially created tape (on a VAX, created with SYS$UPDATE:STABACKIT.COM) or from CD (on a VAX or an Alpha) for the purpose of disk backup. Only the BACKUP tool is loaded into memory, not OpenVMS; hence no disk files are open. Historically, this option was necessary to back up the system disk, but more recent versions of OpenVMS have options that permit backups of any disk during normal operations.

The value of a standalone backup is that the system is in a known, quiescent state. When backing up an operating system disk on a running system, some files will be open (e.g., the printer queues), and the queue manager database files that are backed up are a snapshot of a dynamic state of those files. Normally, backup of a running system is acceptable and, indeed, desirable because the system is expected to be accessible and operational 100 percent of the time. BACKUP is discussed in Chapter 6.

Shutdown

Shutting down the system or shutting down a single cluster node in the system is done with a script called SYS$SYSTEM:SHUTDOWN.COM; however, the most common reason for a shutdown is to accommodate changes made to xVMSSYS.PAR either automatically with AUTOGEN or manually with SYSMAN PARAMETER. If AUTOGEN is used, the system shutdown script is optionally executed.

The SHUTDOWN script permits the operator (or system manager) to inform the users of a pending shutdown and then gracefully shut down. In particular, if continuously running applications (with open databases) need to be informed of a shutdown, this is the recommended mechanism to use.

SYS$MANAGER:SYSHUTDWN.COM is called by SHUTDOWN.COM and is tailored by the system manager for site-specific tasks. Normally, it should mirror the startup script by undoing installs and mounts in the reverse order. In a clustered system, SYSHUTDWN can be coded to be node specific (i.e., to shut down certain processes only on the node on which they are running). The SHUTDOWN dialog is similar to the following:

```
$ @SYS$SYSTEM:SHUTDOWN
SHUTDOWN -- Perform an Orderly System Shutdown
How many minutes until final shutdown [0]: 10
Reason for shutdown: [Standalone] MONTHLY PREVENTIVE MAINTENANCE
Do you want to spin down the disk volumes [No]?
Do you want to invoke the site-specific shutdown procedure [Yes]?
Should an automatic system reboot be performed [No]?
When will the system be rebooted [later]? 12:30
Shutdown options (enter as a comma-separated list):
   REMOVE_NODE     Remaining nodes in the cluster should adjust quorum
   CLUSTER_SHUTDOWN  Entire cluster is shutting down
```

```
REBOOT_CHECK     Check existence of basic system files
SAVE_FEEDBACK     Save AUTOGEN feedback information from this boot
DISABLE_AUTOSTART  Disable autostart queues
Shutdown options [NONE]
```

This causes the following message to be displayed on all user displays to permit users to complete their work before the shutdown event:

```
SHUTDOWN message on BEAVER, from user SYSTEM at _BEAVER$OPA0: 12:00:00.20
BEAVER will shut down in 10 minutes; back up 12:30. Please log off node
BEAVER.
MONTHLY PREVENTIVE MAINTENANCE
```

Countdown messages are sent out to users as well. A similar message is recorded in the operator's log, SYS$MANAGER:OPERATOR.LOG. All operator messages are stored in that file as a log and for security purposes.

Alternately, the operator or manager can shut down the entire cluster with a single command. Using SYSMAN, the SHUTDOWN script is invoked on each node with the specified parameters automatically:

```
$ RUN SYS$SYSTEM:SYSMAN
SYSMAN> SET ENVIRONMENT/CLUSTER
%SYSMAN-I-ENV, current command environment:
  Clusterwide on local cluster
  Username SYSTEM will be used on nonlocal nodes
SYSMAN> SHUTDOWN NODE/CLUSTER_SHUTDOWN/MINUTES_TO_SHUTDOWN=10
_SYSMAN> /AUTOMATIC_REBOOT/REASON="Cluster Reconfiguration"
%SYSMAN-I-SHUTDOWN, SHUTDOWN request sent to node
```

If SHUTDOWN does not work for some reason, there is an immediate (also called *emergency*) shutdown executable called SYS$SYSTEM:OPCCRASH (OPerator Console CRASH), which stops the node without warning or grace. Cached data and print jobs may be lost when using this option, so it should be used with great care. OPCCRASH produces a crash dump, which is written to disk for later analysis.

Booting after Crash

It may be desirable to examine the crash dump after rebooting the system. This step can be automated within the startup script with ANALYZE/CRASH_DUMP. Doing this immediately on restartup ensures that a new dump does not overwrite the previous dump yet to be analyzed. Information in that analysis might be used to determine (and possibly correct) the root cause of the crash, to investigates the causes of system failure and debugs kernel-mode code, such as a device driver. The system manager should have some knowledge of OpenVMS data structures to properly interpret the results of system dump analyzer (SDA) commands.

System and Crash Dump Analysis

When a fatal hardware or software error causes OpenVMS failure, it copies the contents of memory to a system dump file and records the hardware context of all the processors into that file as well. This overwrites the previous dump in that file. When the computer is booted again, processing of the dump file differs according to the architecture. On a VAX, certain data about the failure is written into CLUE$OUTPUT:CLUE$HISTORY.DATA. That information can be viewed in the following example:

```
$ CLUE/DISPLAY

# Node    Time                  Type        Process Name    Module

  1 LOON     4-SEP-2002 09:28 OPERATOR     SYSTEM          UNKNOWN
  2 BEAVER 31-AUG-2002 18:12 OPERATOR     SYSTEM          UNKNOWN
  3 BEAVER 31-AUG-2002 17:58 OPERATOR     SYSTEM          UNKNOWN
  4 OTTER  11-JUN-2002 11:29 OPERATOR     SYSTEM          UNKNOWN
```

To give you an introduction about how rich this command is, look at the first-level help output:

```
CLUE_DISPLAY >help

CLUE

  /DISPLAY

     /DISPLAY = display_command/quals..  filename

     The display module of CLUE reads the specified CLUE History file,
     generated by the CLUE/BINARY command, and prompts for user action.
     A number of commands, as listed below, are available to the user
     from the "CLUE_DISPLAY >" prompt. These commands may also be given
     as a value with /DISPLAY from the DCL command line, for example:

     CLUE/DISPLAY=DIR/SINCE=1-JAN/OUT=TMP.LIS CLUE$HISTORY.DATA.

     If no filename is specified, the default filename is
     CLUE$HISTORY.DATA.

  Additional information available:

     DIRECTORY  SHOW      EXTRACT    DELETE     EXIT

  CLUE /DISPLAY Subtopic?
```

On an Alpha, a one-line summary is added to SYS$ERRORLOG:CLUE$HISTORY.DAT, and extensive information about the failure is written SYS$ERRORLOG: CLUE$*node_ddmmyy_hhmm*.LIS. These two files are in simple ASCII format and can be displayed with TYPE, as illustrated. Only part of the files is displayed in these examples:

```
$ type clue$history.dat /page

Date             Vers System/CPU        Node   Bugcheck  Process    PC
                                                                        Module
---------------- ---- ------------------ ----- --------  ---------  --------
                                                                        ----------------
 8-JAN-1999 11:48 V7.1 DEC 2000 Model 300 EAGLE  CLUEXIT  NULL       801A82A4
                                                                        SYS$CLUSTER
11-JAN-1999 10:38 V7.1 DEC 2000 Model 300 EAGLE  CLUEXIT  NULL       801A82A4
                                                                        SYS$CLUSTER
16-FEB-1999 19:00 V7.1 DEC 2000 Model 300 EAGLE  CLUEXIT  NULL       801A82A4
                                                                        SYS$CLUSTER
22-OCT-1999 01:18 V7.1 DEC 2000 Model 300 EAGLE  CLUEXIT  NULL       801A82A4
                                                                        SYS$CLUSTER
28-MAR-2002 17:40 V7.1 DEC 2000 Model 300 EAGLE  CLUEXIT  CONFIGURE  801B6448
                                                                        SYS$CLUSTER
29-MAR-2002 07:36 V7.1 DEC 2000 Model 300 EAGLE  PROCGONE STARTUP    8664E820
                                                                        IMAGE_MANAGEMENT


$ type CLUE$EAGLE_290302_0736.LIS /page

OpenVMS (TM) Alpha Operating System, Version V7.1 -- System Dump Analysis
                                                     29-MAR-2002 07:36:37.81


Crashdump Summary Information:

Crash Time:         29-MAR-2002 07:36:37.81
Bugcheck Type:      PROCGONE, Process not in system
Node:               EAGLE   (Clustered)
CPU Type:           DEC 2000 Model 300
VMS Version:        V7.1
Current Process:    STARTUP
Current Image:      <not available>
Failing PC:         FFFFFFFF.8664E820     IMAGE_MANAGEMENT_PRO+0A820
Failing PS:         18000000.00000001
Module:             IMAGE_MANAGEMENT
Offset:             00012820

Boot Time:          29-MAR-2002 07:36:09.00
System Uptime:              0 00:00:28.81
Crash/Primary CPU: 00/00
System/CPU Type:    0602
Saved Processes:    3
Pagesize:           8 KByte (8192 bytes)
Physical Memory:    256 MByte (32768 PFNs, contiguous memory)
Dumpfile Pagelets: 12459 blocks
Dump Flags:         writecomp,errlogcomp,dump_style
Dump Type:          compressed,selective
EXE$GL_FLAGS:       poolpging,init,bugdump
Paging Files:       1 Pagefile and 1 Swapfile installed
```

In either case, the dump file should be saved for later analysis by Compaq/HP
personnel. This can be done with the COPY command, but Compaq/HP recommends
that SDA be used instead. By default, the dump file, SYS$SYSTEM:SYSDUMP.DMP, is
never backed up by BACKUP. Use the following on either a VAX or Alpha system:

```
$ANALYZE/CRASH
SDA> COPY SAVEDUMP.DMP
```

A more extensive examination of the dump can be performed with ANALYZE/
CRASH at a later time if necessary. SDA has about 20 commands to display
symbolically (e.g., most of the OpenVMS data structures, such as process

management, memory management, lock management, cluster management, multiprocessor synchronization). Other displays are available as well, for instance:

- Display the contents of a specific process stack.

- Display the call frame.

- Read the OpenVMS global variables and display them.

- Display device status.

- Validate the integrity of queue links.

It should be pointed out that OpenVMS is different internally on the two architectures not only because of the obvious RISC/CISC differences, but also because the method of mapping virtual to physical addresses and I/O structures is different. For instance, to convert virtual space to physical space, the VAX uses two mapping tables, which involves 512-byte pages. But to accommodate the much larger address space of the Alpha, it has three mapping tables, involving 8,192-byte pages.

Furthermore, features have been added to OpenVMS Alpha but not to OpenVMS VAX, such as context switching of process threads. This feature is intended to take better advantage of advanced symmetric multiprocessing (SMP) on the Alpha. Dump processing illustrates differences between OpenVMS as implemented on the VAX versus its implementation on the Alpha. Even though SDA is used in both cases, the two tools are distinct on the two architectures. There is a separate manual for each architecture to describe how this tool works.

In addition to crash analysis, the running system can also be examined. There are two commands, ANALYZE/CRASH (to examine a crash dump) and ANALYZE/SYSTEM (to examine a running system), and both use SDA.

For OpenVMS on VAX systems, the crash log utility extractor (CLUE) is automatically run when the system is booted if the system crashed previously. This supports a CLUE history file, which contains key system parameters pertaining to the crash. The system manager may access this database with CLUE at any time to review crashes. The database is called CLUE$OUTPUT:CLUE$HISTORY.DATA. CLUE is documented in the *OpenVMS System Management Utilities Reference Manual*. SDA is documented in the *OpenVMS VAX System Dump Analyzer Utility Manual*.

OpenVMS on Alpha systems does not run CLUE automatically, and ANALYZE/CRASH_DUMP (or SDA, as it is called in some documents) must be used, as indicated previously. ANALYZE/CRASH is documented in the *OpenVMS DCL Dictionary* and in the *OpenVMS Alpha System Analysis Tools Manual*. CLUE is called from SDA.

Summary

- There are five site-specific startup files the system manager may want to modify. SYS$MANAGER:SYLOGICALS.COM and SYS$MANAGER:SYSTARTUP_VMS.COM are the most commonly modified.

- SYS$MANAGER:SYSHUTDWN.COM is commonly modified by the manager for orderly shutdown of the system.

- SYS$SYSTEM:OPCCRASH.EXE is used for emergency shutdown. This creates a crash dump as well.

- A crash dump is produced whenever OpenVMS encounters an unexpected hardware or software situation.

- A crash dump is examined with ANALYZE/CRASH_DUMP.

- OpenVMS internals differ on the two architectures.

References

1. The *OpenVMS DCL Dictionary* is an unlikely title for the manual that describes all of the DCL commands and their options. It includes numerous examples as well.

2. The *OpenVMS Alpha System Analysis Tools Manual* details the Alpha implementation of SDA.

3. The *OpenVMS VAX System Dump Analyzer Utility Manual* details the VAX implementation of SDA.

4. A detailed description of OpenVMS data structures is found in "the book of Ruth," *Internals and Data Structures* by Ruth Goldenberg et al. The title is preceded by either *VAX/VMS* or *OpenVMS*, depending on the edition. This book is republished often to keep up with newer editions of OpenVMS. The latest complete VAX/VMS edition is for Version 5.5-2. The latest complete Alpha/VMS edition is for Version 1.5. The Alpha edition is partially updated and will continue to be updated.

5. Baldwin's *OpenVMS System Management Guide* is a concise yet complete description of the *System Manager's Manual*.

Chapter 3 — Licenses

OpenVMS has the capability to:

- Register and load licenses.

- Display licenses.

- Unload and delete licenses.

Unlike most UNIX systems, the licensed OpenVMS operating system is bare bones (i.e., to be fully functional, additional licenses must be purchased to create a useful system). For instance, TCP/IP, programming languages, SMP, clustering, file serving, HTTPD server, disk shadowing, and Motif (X Windows) must be licensed explicitly. This scheme means that the manager only has to pay for the features that are used. So, if the machine is to be only a server and no software development is anticipated, no language license needs to be purchased. The system manager can tailor the licenses (thus, the support level and costs) to the intended use of the machine.

All OpenVMS software requires a license, except user-supported freeware. For the purpose of initializing the system, however, the system manager may run from the console without a license. License requirements vary according to the type of CPU on which its associated software will run. Requirements also vary according to the intended usage. The order number for each product licensed by Compaq is found in the software product description (SPD) of the appropriate version of OpenVMS. Specifically, to run OpenVMS on a single CPU with interactive users, two licenses must be loaded:

1. Operating System Base License, which permits one login from the console

2. OpenVMS Concurrent-Use License, specifying how many simultaneous users are permitted to log in

If the computer has multiple CPUs—that is, symmetric multiprocessing (SMP)—one more license for each additional CPU is also required:

3. Symmetric Multiprocessing (SMP) Base Extension

When installing additional products, the system manager must consult the product's SPD to determine what license options are available. The OpenVMS Base with a Concurrent-Use License includes the following:

- Several editors

- MAIL client

- Java language and run-time support (Alpha only)

- MACRO (assembly language) Compiler

- POSIX Threads library

- Visual Threads tool to analyze multithread applications

- Librarian utility

- Hypersort library of APIs

- Symbolic debugger for application development

- System code debugger for driver development

- Record Management System (RMS) File utilities

- Availability Manager, a tool to monitor OpenVMS nodes from a PC

- Management Station, a tool to manage certain aspects of OpenVMS from a PC

- Batch and Print queuing

- Accounting utility

- Backup utility

- Kerberos security/authentication

- Compaq Secure Web Server (CSWS), based on the Apache server

- Extensible Markup Language (XML)

- Netscape FastTrack Server

- E-business packages, such as Enterprise Directory, Reliable Transaction Router, and Microsoft's Component Object Model (COM)

But several useful tools and applications are licensed separately:

- TCP/IP

- Disk shadowing and striping (RAID 0, 1, and 5)

- Compilers

- Symmetric multiprocessing (SMP)

- Clustering

- NSF (also called PATHWORKS or Advanced Server) server

- DECwindows Motif

One of the network application support (NAS) licenses should probably be loaded as well. There are several NAS licenses, and they are designed to combine commonly required networking licenses. For instance:

NAS Base Server 200 includes licenses for:

- DECwindows, Motif

- DECprint Supervisor (DCPS)

- DECnet and DECnet-Plus

- PATHWORKS

- TCP/IP Services

NAS Production Server 400 includes licenses for the above plus:

- DECforms

- DEC Distributed Queuing Service

- ACMS

- Reliable Transaction Router (RTR)

- RMS Journaling

- VMScluster Software

- Volume Shadowing

These licenses can be upgraded as well. For instance, if the manager finds that the NAS 200 does not include enough licenses, it can be upgraded to NAS 400.

The OpenVMS SPD also lists freeware that runs on OpenVMS. Here is a brief list:

- WWW browsers: Netscape and Mosaic supported by Motif. LYNX is a character cell, text-based browser.

- WWW Servers: Ohio State University supported. CERN also has one.

- perl: a scripting language used on UNIX

- GNU sed: a UNIX stream editor

- tcl: another stream editor, and tk, an X Windows system toolkit for tcl

- yacc and bison: compiler-compilers

- grep: a regular expression search engine

- News readers: ANU NEWS, VNEWS, MXRN/DXRN, NEWSRDR

- MPEG video player

- IUPOP3: an e-mail server

- Pine: an e-mail and news client

- MX: an e-mail server

- Various HTML tools to syntax check and convert HTML files

- Motif and X Windows tools and utilities

Licensing today is based on a three-tier model: enterprise, departmental, and workstation. For instance, the Alpha enterprise system class includes the following:

- DEC 4000 series

- DEC 7000 series

- DEC 10000 series

- AlphaServer 8200, Compaq AlphaServer GS60

- AlphaServer 8400, Compaq AlphaServer GS140

- Compaq AlphaServer GS160, GS320

Software License

Compaq/HP software is never purchased. Instead, Compaq/HP grants a license to use the software. The license agreement must be signed by the using organization, and Compaq/HP will issue a product authorization kit (PAK). The information in the PAK is managed by the OpenVMS license management facility (LMF). LMF supports five types of licenses: availability, activity, personal use, user, and group.

- *Availability* provides for limited uses (not user) for the machine type.

- *Activity* provides for a specified limit of uses on the system.

- *Personal Use* is keyed to unlimited use by specific users, usually for a limited amount of time.

- *User* provides for limited user access.

- *Group* authorizes access to a group of products, usually related. A Group license is also one of the other four: Availability, Activity, Personal Use, or User.

Entering a license is a two-step process:

- *Registering the license.* The variables from the PAK are entered into the permanent database.

- *Loading the product.* The license must be moved from the permanent database to the volatile one. This step is normally done when the computer is booted.

Products that require licenses access only the volatile database, not the permanent database. The permanent database contains a history of changes made to a given license as well as all of the PAK data. A typical PAK for volume shadowing would resemble the following information:

```
              ISSUER: DEC
AUTHORIZATION NUMBER: ALS-WM-45789-6666
        PRODUCT NAME: VOLSHAD
            PRODUCER: DEC
     NUMBER OF UNITS: 400
             VERSION: 7.3
PRODUCT RELEASE DATE:
KEY TERMINATION DATE: 31-DEC-2001
AVAILABILITY TABLE CODE: E
   ACTIVITY TABLE CODE:
         KEY OPTIONS: MOD_UNITS
       PRODUCT TOKEN:
        HARDWARE I.D.:
            CHECKSUM: 2-EBID-GOOD-NIGH-OJJG
```

An OpenVMS License specifies two key quantities: availability and activity. *Availability* refers to the CPU "horsepower," such that more powerful CPUs require more units of availability. *Activity* (called *Units* on the PAK) refers to the number of concurrent uses (not users) of the product. Uses are counted because many products can be activated through network and batch access as well as interactive access.

To display the particular computer's License Unit Requirement Table (LURT), use the following SHOW command:

```
MANAGER> show license/unit
VMS/LMF Charge Information for node BEAVER
This is a VAXstation 4000-90A, hardware model type 475

Type: A,  * Not Permitted *      (VMS Capacity)
Type: B,  * Not Permitted *      (VMS Server)
Type: C,  * Not Permitted *      (VMS Concurrent User)
Type: D,  Units Required: 100    (VMS Workstation)
Type: E,  Units Required: 50     (System Integrated Products)
Type: F,  Units Required: 10     (Layered Products)
Type: G,  * Not Permitted *      (VMS Reserved)
Type: H,  * Not Permitted *      (Alpha Layered Products)
Type: I,  Units Required: 10     (Layered Products)
```

Notice that the command shows not only the Units assigned to the computer, but also the computer's general characteristics.

Now, to tie the PAK and UNIT_REQUIREMENTS together: The PAK states AVAILABILITY TABLE CODE: E. The LURT shows UNIT_REQUIREMENTS for TYPE: E is 50. This is well under the PAK's NUMBER OF UNITS of 400, hence the license PAK for volume shadowing would be valid on this machine. If the number of units in the PAK is greater than required, the remainder will be shared across other nodes in the cluster automatically, or the system manager can designate which nodes are to be licensed.

The entire cluster's LURT can be displayed easily, as follows. This display conveniently shows the sum of the LURTs throughout the cluster, where EAGLE is an Alpha and the other three are VAXes:

```
MANAGER> show license/unit/cluster
VMS/LMF Cluster License Unit Requirements Information    8-SEP-2002
17:33:37.11

   Node              A     B     C     D     E     F     G     H     I
BEAVER               -     -     -   100    50    10     -     -    10
EAGLE               12     -     -     -     -     -     -  1050  1050
LOON                 -     -     -   100    50    10     -     -    10
CSWWW                -   100     -     -    50    10     -     -    10

Total Cluster Unit Requirements
Type: A, Units Required:       12  (VMS Capacity)
Type: B, Units Required:      100  (VMS Server)
Type: C,   * Not Permitted *       (VMS Concurrent User)
Type: D, Units Required:      200  (VMS Workstation)
Type: E, Units Required:      150  (VMS System Integrated Products)
Type: F, Units Required:       30  (Layered Products)
Type: G,   * Not Permitted *       (VMS Reserved)
Type: H, Units Required:     1050  (Alpha Layered Products)
Type: I, Units Required:     1080  (Layered Products)
```

Once the computer's LURT requirements are checked against the PAK, the next step is to register, enable, and load the license (i.e., to enter the PAK into the license database and activate it). This is commonly done with an OpenVMS script:

```
$ @SYS$UPDATE:VMSLICENSE
```

which presents a menu to the manager that resembles the following. The manager should select option 1 to register the PAK, answering the remaining questions as they are presented. These questions are not shown, but generally data from each line of the PAK is requested. Registering a new PAK automatically enables it, and loading the PAK is a user option.

```
VMS License Management Utility Options:

    1. REGISTER a Product Authorization Key
    2. AMEND an existing Product Authorization Key
    3. CANCEL an existing Product Authorization Key
    4. LIST the Product Authorization Keys
    5. MODIFY an existing Product Authorization Key
    6. DISABLE an existing Product Authorization Key
    7. DELETE an existing Product Authorization Key
    8. COPY an existing Product Authorization Key
    9. MOVE an existing Product Authorization Key
   10. ENABLE an existing Product Authorization Key
   11. SHOW the licenses loaded on this node
   12. SHOW the unit requirements for this node

   99. EXIT this procedure

Type '?' at any prompt for a description of the information
requested.  Press Ctrl/Z at any prompt to return to this menu.

Enter one of the above choices [1]:
```

Alternately, the LICENSE command can be used, but this is not a novice tool nor is it particularly intuitive. The VMSLICENSE script (or the LICENSE command) offers many other options to manage the license database. These include deleting licenses and assigning licenses to specific nodes in a cluster or to specific users, but details of these operations are beyond the intent of this book.

Software Installation

The final step is to install the software using either the script, VMSINSTAL, or the DCL command, PRODUCT (also called POLYCENTER). Read the installation instructions that accompany the product to determine the exact procedure and other requirements. Normally, options must be selected, and the manager should do his or her homework before installation. This is a typical PRODUCT installation dialog when installing TCP/IP:

```
$ PRODUCT INSTALL TCPIP

The following products have been selected:
DEC AXPVMS TCPOP V5.1-0 Layered Product

Choose one or more items from the menu separated by commas: 1

The following product has been selected:
DEC VAXVMS TCPIP V5.1-0 Layered Product

Do you want to continue? [YES]

Configuration phase starting ...

You will be asked to choose options, if any, for each selected product
and for any products that may be installed to satisfy software dependency
requirements.

DEC VAXVMS TCPIP V5.1-0: Compaq TCP/IP Services for OpenVMS.
(c) Compaq Computer Corporation 2000. All Rights Reserved.
Compaq Computer Corporation
Compaq TCP/IP Services for OpenVMS offers several license options.

Do you want the defaults for all options? [YES]

Do you want to review the options? [NO]

Execution phase starting ...
The following product will be installed to destination:
DEC VAXVMS TCPIP V5.1-0 DISK$OVMSVAXSYS:[VMS$COMMON.]

Portion done: 0%...10%...20%...30%...40%...50%...60%...70%...80%...90%
%PCSI-I-PRCOUTPUT, output from subprocess follows ...
% TCPIP-W-PCSI_INSTALL
% - Execute SYS$MANAGER:TCPIP$CONFIG.COM to proceed with configuration of
% Compaq TCP/IP Services.
%

Portion done: 100%

The following product has been installed:
DEC VAXVMS TCPIP V5.1-0 Layered Product

DEC VAXVMS TCPIP T5.1-0: Compaq TCP/IP Services for OpenVMS.

Check the release notes for current status of the product.
```

Summary

Software licensing is constantly changing. Licenses issued years ago have been
superseded (e.g., the ClusterWide license of the 1980s does not exist any more). Also,
licenses for older technology (e.g., a VAX or an early Alpha server) do not apply to
newer machines (e.g., an OpenVMS Base license must be formally transferred via
Compaq/HP from machine to machine). This phenomenon will never go away,

because technology is always changing. In view of changing licensing requirements, Compaq/HP must be contacted to find out how older licenses can be applied to newer software.

- The License database location is defined by the logical, LMF$LICENSE.

- The product authorization key (PAK) contains the information that is loaded into the license database.

- LICENSE is used to manage the license database.

- $SYSMAN LICENSE can be used to manage licenses on more than one node.

- LICENSE is used to display the permanent license database.

- SHOW LICENSE displays the licenses that are currently active (loaded) on a particular CPU in the volatile database.

- @SYS$UPDATE:VMSLICENSE is an interactive command file to assist the system manager in maintaining the license database.

- The License Unit Requirement Table (LURT) specifies the number of units required by the CPU. It is in SYS$SYSTEM:LMF$LURT.DAT.

- The software product description (SPD) for the product describes the license requirements and ordering information.

Related Publications

1. The *OpenVMS License Management Utility Manual* includes a description of the LICENSE command as well.

2. *Software Product Description* of a product describes its general capabilities and detailed specifics regarding supporting software and hardware.

3. License units required for all VAXes and Alphas can be found online at www.compaq.com/products/software/info in the Reference Material tab. A typical entry looks like this:

```
System Model      System      Units   Layered Product Units
AlphaServer 4000  1 CPU        400                    1100
                  2 CPU        500                    1100
                  3 CPU        600                    1100
                  4 CPU        700                    1100
```

Chapter 4 — User Accounts, Login, and Accounting

OpenVMS has the capability to:

- Create, modify, display, and delete user accounts.

- Manage the several global parameters governing login security policy.

- Monitor account usage and produce a wide variety of reports.

Before a user can log into an OpenVMS system, he or she must have an account. The most secure way to manage an OpenVMS system is to assign unique accounts to each user. Protected in this way, a user may be assured that his or her files are private and can be accessed only by permission. By default, all files created in an account are private; however, the user may choose to share files with other users, and that discussion is found in Chapter 8.

Accounts have other characteristics as well. These characteristics govern how system resources are allocated to the user when logged in. There are more than a dozen quota limits associated with each account. The quota values are measured by OpenVMS to enforce overall performance of the system. For instance, the number of memory-resident pages (OpenVMS is a demand paging system) is limited so that a single user cannot allocate all of physical memory to his or her executing image. As with security settings, the default quotas assigned at account creation are usually adequate, but the system manager (not the user) may change them. These characteristics are similar to, but much more extensive than, the ones that the UNIX limit and ulimit commands govern.

Creating an account and then assigning and supervising its quotas is a system manager task. The importance of this task is more completely described in this chapter.

Account Management

Account management is important. I've see UNIX administrators simply use an editor to copy/paste an entry into the passwd file and create a new account. There is no similar concept in OpenVMS. To create a user account, the manager must perform the following:

- Create the account with appropriate privileges using AUTHORIZE.

- Create a root directory on the device specified by the account using CREATE/DIR.

- Possibly (depending on user sophistication) create an account subdirectory for mail messages, also using CREATE/DIR.

- If quotas are active on the user's disk, allocate disk quota for the account using SYSMAN DISKQUOTA.

SYS$SYSTEM:SYSUAF.DAT (UAF means user authorization file) contains the authorization profile for all users. This file is similar in function, but not in form, to UNIX's passwd file. The format of the SYSUAF was partially illustrated in the ANALYZE/RMS example in Chapter 2. There are several parts to the OpenVMS profile; some are obvious and others are peculiar to OpenVMS. This is a complete list:

- *User identification data*: real name, user name, initial password, user identification code (UIC) (a security artifact), and account name (for accounting)

- *Account default data*: login directory, login command file name (normally called LOGIN.COM)

- *Login attribute data*: login time for network and batch, mail attributes, login message action, password characteristics (e.g., length, lifetime), account enabled or disabled

- Quotas limit data described as follows.

- Privilege data, described in Chapter 8, defines which system utilities the user may access.

- Identifier data, described in Chapter 8, defines the user's security groups. This feature is similar to the UNIX group.

The SYSUAF.DAT is not a public file and is available only to SYSTEM. It is accessed via installed images only (see Chapter 8). Hence, a UNIX-like "crack" function cannot be performed on OpenVMS by a user with nominal privileges. There are rumors that such a function exists on OpenVMS, but because the account file is not public, a cracker cannot be used. If the hacker has SYSTEM privileges, there is no need for a cracker. Naturally, the user password (or passwords; OpenVMS supports a two-password login option) is encrypted before it is stored in the SYSUAF.DAT, and it is stored in binary and cannot be displayed. There is no known decryption algorithm, so even the system manager cannot discover a user's password.

A typical dialog the system manager could use to perform the aforementioned steps would look like this:

```
$ RUN SYS$SYSTEM:AUTHORIZE
```

```
UAF> ADD JONES/PASSWORD=LPB57WM/UIC=[014,1] -
_UAF> /DEVICE=DISK$USER/DIRECTORY=[JONES] -
_UAF> /LGICMD=DISK$USER:[JONES]LOGIN -
_UAF> /OWNER="ROBERT JONES"/ACCOUNT=DOC
UAF> EXIT

$ CREATE/DIRECTORY DISK$USER:[JONES] /OWNER_UIC=[014,1]

$ CREATE/DIRECTORY DISK$USER:[JONES.MAIL] /OWNER_UIC=[014,1]

$ RUN SYS$SYSTEM:SYSMAN
  SYSMAN> DISKQUOTA ADD  -
_SYSMAN> [JONES]/DEVICE=DISK$USER/PERMQUOTA=2000 -
_SYSMAN> /OVERDRAFT=500
  SYSMAN> EXIT
```

Clearly, such a complex series of commands is laborious and prone to typos. Hence, it should be mechanized via a script. Usually, the system manager creates a command file similar to SYS$EXAMPLES:ADDUSER.COM (supplied in the OpenVMS delivery) to perform the previous steps interactively. This way the manager avoids mistakes and speeds up the process of creating new accounts. The new system manager would probably copy SYS$EXAMPLES:ADDUSER.COM to the SYS$SYSTEM directory and modify it to enforce local site policies. For instance, the command file may be coded to use the user's name to initialize the password. To appreciate the complexity of the SYSUAF.DAT, here is a display of all information for a single user. Notice that AUTHORIZE changes the prompt to UAF>:

```
$ mcr authorize
UAF> show dmiller/full

Username: DMILLER                      Owner:  DAVID MILLER
Account:                               UIC:    [20,4] ([DMILLER])
CLI:      DCL                          Tables: DCLTABLES
Default:  FACULTY:[DMILLER]
LGICMD:   FACULTY:[DMILLER]LOGIN.COM
Flags:  DisCtlY
Primary days:   Mon Tue Wed Thu Fri
Secondary days:                Sat Sun
No access restrictions
Expiration:        (none)     Pwdminimum:  6  Login Fails:   0
Pwdlifetime:        90 00:00  Pwdchange:  22-MAY-2002 09:19
Last Login:  1-AUG-2002 21:15 (interactive), 20-AUG-2001 17:20 (non-interactive)
Maxjobs:          10  Fillm:        100  Bytlm:        50000
Maxacctjobs:       0  Shrfillm:       0  Pbytlm:           0
Maxdetach:         0  BIOlm:        100  JTquota:       4096
Prclm:             5  DIOlm:        100  WSdef:          500
Prio:              4  ASTlm:        200  WSquo:         5000
Queprio:           0  TQElm:         10  WSextent:     10000
CPU:          (none)  Enqlm:       4000  Pgflquo:      50000
Authorized Privileges:
  NETMBX    TMPMBX
Default Privileges:
  NETMBX    TMPMBX
Identifier                   Value          Attributes
```

This book will not describe each of the previous fields in any detail. I merely want to impress on the reader that the system manager has a great deal of latitude when defining what a user may be permitted to do; however, this is a good time to point out another OpenVMS deviation from UNIX. By default, OpenVMS passwords are aged (see PWLIFETIME and PWDCHANGE in the previous display).

Data that is not supplied in the ADD command is copied from an account called DEFAULT, which has a UIC of [200,200]. This account is not meant to be used in the traditional sense (no one can log into DEFAULT), but merely to supply default values for newly created accounts. The manager may find it necessary to adjust quotas in DEFAULT to more closely match the requirements of the site (e.g., if all users will be using Motif, several quotas must be increased). These quotas are listed in the installation guide.

Accounts can also be created and managed from a Windows NT workstation with OpenVMS Management Station, as documented in *OpenVMS Management Station Overview and Release Notes*. There is little published user documentation on this program, because the application's HELP files substitute for documents.

There is a freeware GUI Motif interface to replace AUTHORIZE as well. It is called DWprofile and is found at www.multimania.com/pmoreau/decw/xutils.html. Although published in 1992, it works fine on today's systems as well. In fact, OpenVMS is well known for its backward compatibility support of software.

Once a user's account has been established, the system manager will probably not have to access it again; however, the most common reason for revisiting AUTHORIZE is to reset the password, because the user cannot remember it. This is done with the following command:

```
$ AUTHORIZE
UAF> MODIFY/PASSWORD=FORGETMENOT username
```

Then the user logs in under this new password. After successful login, the user will be immediately forced to change the password because, by default, any password change made by the manager is immediately expired.

If the user wants to change his or her password, the command is SET PASSWORD. This command works like the UNIX passwd command by interrogating the user for the old password and the new password. Likewise, when the user's password expires, a new password dialog takes place at login time.

Login.com

The user's SYSUAF.DAT entry specifies a script to be executed whenever login is performed. In the previous example (i.e., UAF> SHOW DMILLER/FULL), it is the LGICMD parameter. In this case, LOGIN.COM corresponds to .profile in UNIX, although that name is not reserved in OpenVMS. In Windows NT, a script's file name is defined in the user's profile and stored embedded in the system directory on the domain server.

After logging in (or within LOGIN.COM), the user may customize his or her session by defining such things as:

- OpenVMS prompt (see SET PROMPT)

- Terminal characteristics (see SET TERMINAL)

- Shortcut keys (see DEFINE/KEY)

- File synonyms (see DEFINE)

- Command synonyms (using the string assignment to define symbols)

For instance, to change the prompt from "$" to "MANAGER>", the following is used:

```
$ SET PROMPT="MANAGER> "
```

If the logical SYS$SYLOGIN is defined (it is usually equated to SYS$MANAGER:SYLOGIN.COM), then this command file is executed each time a user logs in but before the user's LOGIN.COM. That way the system manager can create universal symbols and logicals to be used by all users. The user's LOGIN.COM may override those predefined definitions. SYLOGIN.COM is discussed in Chapter 1.

Disk Quota

Disk quotas are device-specific, not universal. Any disk may have quotas enabled. If enabled, each account's disk space usage on that disk is compared with the user's disk quota, and the account is prohibited from using more than this allocated limit. Disk quotas are managed with SYSMAN DISKQUOTA. The quota database is created with the subcommand CREATE, and accounts are added with the subcommand MODIFY. For instance, to establish a disk with quota enabled—and all users of the disk must have a quota defined—the following command is used:

```
$ SYSMAN DISKQUOTA CREATE/DEVICE=disk_name
```

This command is described in the *OpenVMS System Manager's Manual*, Chapter 9. SYSMAN is fully described in the *OpenVMS System Management Utilities Reference Manual*, Chapter 21.

Next, the manager would define a disk quota for the specific user:

```
$ SYSMAN DISKQUOTA ADD [DMILLER]/DEVICE=FACULTY -
```

```
_$ /PERMQUOTA=150000/OVERDRAFT=100
```

This command was illustrated previously as well. The user can monitor personal disk usage with the simple command, shown as follows:

```
$ show quo
  User [DMILLER] has 90821 blocks used, 59179 available,
  of 150000 authorized and permitted overdraft of 100 blocks on FACULTY
```

Likewise, the manager can monitor disk quota, as in the following example:

```
$ mcr sysman
SYSMAN> diskquota show [dmiller] /device=faculty

disk quota statistics on device EAGLE$DKB0:[FACULTY.] --
Node LOON
     UIC               Usage        Permanent Quota   Overdraft Limit
  [DMILLER]            90821        150000            100
```

Notice that disk quota is not directly tied to user authorization and needs to be managed separately. The disk quota database is maintained on the target disk in [000000]QUOTA.SYS. It is also possible to add disk quota management to a disk at any time (i.e., after directories have been established). This is done with the following command:

```
$ SYSMAN DISKQUOTA REBUILD/DEVICE=disk_name
```

Login Security

The system manager may control (using AUTHORIZE) several parameters that govern the login process. These parameters are specified in the SYSUAF and are listed as follows. The specific AUTHORIZE qualifier is indicated in parentheses. Notice that these qualifiers are defined for every account, and many of them are shown in the previous SHOW DMILLER/FULL example. The parameters are as follows:

- Whether two passwords are required to log in (/PASSWORD=)

- The minimum length of a password (/PWDMINIMUM=)

- The lifetime of a password (i.e., how often the password must be changed) (/PWDLIFETIME=)

- Whether the user is permitted to change his or her password (FLAG=LOCKPWD)

- Whether the user must use system-generated passwords (/GENERATE=)

- What time of day and day of week the user may log in (/ACCESS=)

In addition, certain systemwide policy settings may be controlled (via SYSMAN PARAMETER) by the manager. These settings are stored in xVMSSYS.PAR, as discussed in both Chapters 2 and 7. The following is a partial list of these SYSMAN-pertinent parameters (the specific parameter is listed in parentheses):

- Maximum number of login failures before the user is disconnected (LGI_RETRY_LIM)

- Maximum amount of time the user has to respond to the login prompt before being disconnected (LGI_RETRY_TMO)

- Maximum number of login failures from the same location or to the same account permitted before a break-in event is declared (LGI_BRK_LIM)

- How long to disable further login attempts from that location or to that account (LGI_BRK_TMO)

- When a break-in is detected, the user's account may be disabled (LGI_BRK_DISUSER).

SYSMAN is used to display and change current settings. The following example shows how to list them all. Only the rightmost column requires an explanation. Some parameters take place immediately, which are termed *dynamic*. Other parameters require a system boot before they are effective; these are termed *nondynamic*. The dynamic position of the display is blank for these parameters.

```
$ MCR SYSMAN
SYSMAN> parameter show /lgi
Node BEAVER:    Parameters in use: ACTIVE

Parameter Name      Current    Default    Minimum      Maximum Unit    Dynamic
--------------      -------    -------    -------      ------- ----    -------
LGI_BRK_TERM              1          1          0            1 Boolean       D
LGI_BRK_DISUSER          0          0          0            1 Boolean       D
LGI_PWD_TMO             30         30          0          255 Seconds       D
LGI_RETRY_LIM            3          3          0          255 Tries         D
LGI_RETRY_TMO           20         20          0          255 Seconds       D
LGI_BRK_LIM              5          5          1          255 Failures      D
LGI_BRK_TMO            300        300          0      5184000 Seconds       D
LGI_HID_TIM           300        300          0   1261440000 Seconds       D
```

SYSMAN also includes HELP for all parameters. The following display illustrates this feature. Unfortunately, the command appears a bit baroque, but the information is valuable. It would appear that this value is set incorrectly on my system, because I use LAT.

```
SYSMAN> help parameter parameter lgi_brk_term
PARAMETERS
```

```
Parameters

  LGI_BRK_TERM

      LGI_BRK_TERM causes the terminal name to be part of the
      association string for the terminal mode of break-in detection.
      When off (0), association is done on user name only. LGI_BRK_
      TERM is set by default (1).  It should be cleared if physical
      terminal names are created dynamically (that is, if LAT is
      installed) and effective break-in detection is desired.

      LGI_BRK_TERM is a DYNAMIC parameter.
```

The change requires several commands, because all changes are made in a workspace
and then moved to memory to become active. The changes are also moved to file to
make them permanent. These steps are as follows:

```
SYSMAN> parameter use active          ! initialize workspace
SYSMAN> parameter set lgi_brk_term 0  ! make the change
SYSMAN> parameter write active        ! write workspace to memory
SYSMAN> parameter write current       ! write workspace to file
SYSMAN> parameter sho lgi_brk_term    ! display change

Node BEAVER:   Parameters in use: ACTIVE

Parameter Name      Current   Default   Minimum   Maximum Unit  Dynamic
--------------      -------   -------   -------   ------- ----  -------
LGI_BRK_TERM              0         1         0         1 Boolean     D
```

Accounting

The OpenVMS program which produces accounting reports is called ACCOUNTING.
This powerful program permits the manager to select which items from the
accounting database are to be reported and how to report them. The accounting
database content is controlled by the SET ACCOUNTING command and is usually
specified in the SYSTARTUP_VMS.COM file. The manager may collect any
combination or all of the following:

- Resources used by an image

- Resources used by an unsuccessful attempt to log in

- Resources used by a print job

- Resources used by various process types: batch, detached, interactive, network,
  and subprocess

The SHOW ACCOUNTING command with no qualifiers displays the current
settings. At any time, the ACCOUNTING program may be used to display or print
any portion of the database. For instance, the manager may display all failed logins in

the last 24 hours each morning to check for hacking attempts. First, ensure that login data is collected:

```
$ set account/enable=login
```

Later, the following command can be issued to display details of login failures. The following display has no recognizable user ID; it could be simply a typo or a deliberate break-in attempt. This attempt was made by a user on the LAN (RTA1: is a DECnet device name) from the node named LOON from the SYSTEM account—from one node on the LAN to another. Obviously, I fabricated the attempt for this example:

```
$ account/type=logfail/full
LOGIN FAILURE
-------------
Username:          <login>        UIC:            [SYSTEM]
Account:           <login>        Finish time:    2-AUG-2002 11:29:00.57
Process ID:        20602584       Start time:     2-AUG-2002 11:28:30.66
Owner ID:                         Elapsed time:         0 00:00:29.91
Terminal name:     RTA1:          Processor time:       0 00:00:00.16
Remote node addr:  64518          Priority:       4
Remote node name:  LOON           Privilege <31-00>: 0010C000
Remote ID:         SYSTEM         Privilege <63-32>: 00000000
Remote full name:
Queue entry:                      Final status code: 00D38064
Queue name:
Job name:
Final status text: %LOGIN-F-CMDINPUT, error reading command input

Page faults:          347         Direct IO:              8
Page fault reads:       9         Buffered IO:           41
Peak working set:     390         Volumes mounted:        0
Peak page file:      2333         Images executed:        1
```

I have shown how ACCOUNTING can be used to secure the system. Chapter 8 discusses another program, AUDIT, which can be used in this way as well. ACCOUNTING can also be used for classic chargeback reports based on resources used (e.g., to determine the number of logins by user or the number of pages each user printed during a time period).

Mail Profile

Managing the user's MAIL database is not as involved as managing the account database. For the most part, MAIL takes care of itself. Occasionally, users get into trouble and the manager must intervene. Unfortunately, there are no OpenVMS programs to help the manager; however, a freeware package call MAILUAF does a fine job. With this program, the manager can usually spot the difficulty by displaying the user's mail profile. An example display of DMILLER's profile is as follows, and by using MAILUAF, these values can be changed easily. MAILUAF can be found in Hunter Goatly's OpenVMS software collection at www.process.com/openvms/index.html.

```
MAILUAF> sho dmiller /full

User DMILLER subdirectory is [.MAIL]
User DMILLER has 3 new messages
User DMILLER has not set a forwarding address
User DMILLER personal name is "David Miller"
User DMILLER editor is EDT
User DMILLER has cc prompting disabled
User DMILLER has automatic copies to self disabled
User DMILLER has automatic deleted message purge enabled
User DMILLER default print queue is SYS$PRINT
User DMILLER has not set a default print form
```

The manager may also use this utility to create a mail alias with a forwarding address. For instance, it is customary to have a POSTMASTER mail account. This can be done without creating a special account. Instead, create an entry in the mail profile for POSTMASTER and have it forward all mail to SYSTEM:

```
MAILUAF> ADD POSTMASTER /FORWARD=SYSTEM
MAILUAF> show postmaster
User POSTMASTER forwarding address is SYSTEM
User POSTMASTER has automatic deleted message purge enabled
```

Summary

- SYS$SYSTEM:SYSUAF.DAT is the user authorization file (UAF) in which user names, privileges, and most other user characteristics are stored.

- SYS$SYSTEM:RIGHTSLIST.DAT is the rights list database related to access control lists (ACLs), which are discussed fully in Chapter 8.

- SYS$SYSTEM:AUTHORIZE.EXE is the program to manage SYS$SYSTEM:SYSUAF.DAT and RIGHTSLIST.DAT.

- CREATE is a DCL command to make a directory.

- SYS$SYSTEM:SYSMAN.EXE is a program to manage general login parameters and to manage disk quotas.

- SYS$EXAMPLES:ADDUSER.COM is an interactive command procedure used to create a user account. Normally, this must be moved to SYS$SYSTEM and modified for site-specific needs.

- OpenVMS includes a dictionary of prohibited passwords, and SYS$SYSTEM:LOCAL_PASSWORD_DICTIONARY.DATA is the site-specific extension to this dictionary, which is created and managed by the system manager.

- ACCOUNTING is a program to report system resource utilization that operates on the database in SYS$MANAGER:ACCOUNTNG.DAT.

- SET ACCOUNTING and SHOW ACCOUNTING are the DCL commands that control what is saved in the accounting database.

- The database for users' mail is in SYS$SYSTEM:VMSMAIL_PROFILE.DATA and is managed with various MAIL subcommands, such as SHOW and SET.

Related Publications

1. The definitive OpenVMS security manual is called the *OpenVMS Guide to System Security.*

2. The *OpenVMS System Manager's Manual*, Chapter 7, discusses aser accounts.

3. The various system management utilities referenced in this chapter (i.e., ACCOUNTING, AUTHORIZE, SET, SHOW, and SYSMAN) are described completely in the *OpenVMS System Management Utilities Reference Manual.*

4. *OpenVMS Management Station Overview and Release Notes* includes disk and printer management functions besides account management.

5. The Website www.multimania.com/pmoreau/decw/decw.html is the source of many freeware Motif packages that may interest the system manager.

Chapter 5 — Queues

OpenVMS has the capability to:

- Support both printer queues and batch execution queues.

- Display, modify, delete, requeue, or hold queue entries.

- Start, stop, and display queues.

- Automatically fail-over a single queue manager to an alternate cluster node.

- Automatically convert various file formats to PostScript for PostScript printers.

- Support generic queues, which will automatically redirect print jobs to the first available printer in a printer farm.

- Support print devices, which are attached directly to the computer, connected to PCs, connected to a printer (or terminal) server, or connected directly on a LAN.

Queue management is one of the most difficult aspects of OpenVMS, partly because there are so many options (thus many commands) and because there are often many queues and multiple printers on each queue. The functions and examples in this chapter only scratch the surface of the possibilities. In addition to command-line control, a PC-hosted GUI is available, called the OpenVMS Management Station.[1] Two kinds of queues are supported by OpenVMS: batch and print.

Queue Manager

The queue manager is normally started at boot time, in SYSTARTUP_VMS. It is a clusterwide process that performs all queue management functions for all users logged into the cluster. It operates from a three-file database that records queue characteristics and job information. The files are all in SYS$SYSTEM and called QMAN$MASTER.DAT, SYS$QUEUE_MANAGER.QMAN$JOURNAL, and SYS$QUEUE_MANAGER.QMAN$QUEUES. This database may be assigned to any disk mounted clusterwide through the use of logical definitions. If the node hosting the queue manager is stopped for some reason, the queue manager will automatically and invisibly fail-over to another node in the cluster to provide seamless queuing operations. It is also possible to run up to five queue managers on the cluster when there is a high rate of job (print and/or batch) submissions. The print and batch queue manager (QUEMAN) is started with the following command:

---

1. This GUI also supports account management and disk management.

```
$ START/QUEUE/MANAGER
```

Jobs are added to a batch queue with SUBMIT and to a print queue with PRINT. To display a list of all jobs entered in any queue and its number, a user can enter the following command:

```
$ SHOW ENTRY

Entry  Jobname          Username  Blocks  Status
-----  -------          --------  ------  ------
    1  ONDUTY_Batch     SYSTEM            Holding until 16-SEP-2002 00:05:00
       On generic batch queue SYS$BATCH

    2  DEFRAG_DKA0      SYSTEM            Holding until 17-SEP-2002 00:05:00
       On idle batch queue BEAVER_BATCH

   24  WEEKLY_Batch     SYSTEM            Holding until 17-SEP-2002 00:00:00
       On idle batch queue BEAVER_BATCH

  136  MX_WATCH         SYSTEM            Holding until 15-SEP-2002 19:13:29
       On idle batch queue CSWWW_BATCH
```

A user may delete any of his or her jobs using the entry number shown in the previous list with the command

```
$ DELETE/ENTRY=job_queue_entry
```

Of course, a user can only delete jobs he or she created. The manager can use the following command to show all user jobs in a given queue and delete any of them:

```
$ SHOW QUEUE queue_name
```

Batch Queues

Batch queues act like UNIX background. OpenVMS has no background mode, so instead a user-created job (actually a command file script) is executed at lower-than-interactive priority.[1] Batch jobs are created with the SUBMIT command. This batch mode concept is more in line with the IBM mainframe concept of a batch job. A job submitted to a batch queue may be run on any node in the cluster and may be delayed before execution is begun. The batch job typically takes on the same environment as the submitting user (e.g., privileges and disk environment are the same); however, the user has control of some of these characteristics. Only SYSTEM may create batch jobs on behalf of other users.

Batch queues can be configured to run one job at a time or multiple jobs in parallel. Furthermore, a user may submit multiple jobs to any queue. The manager can create multiple batch queues, and they can be configured to run jobs on a specific node in the

---

1. Alternately, the SPAWN command can be used to create a child process for execution of a script or command. This topic was discussed briefly in Chapter 1.

cluster or on any available node (i.e., the queue manager can do *load leveling*). Creation of a batch queue is performed with a single command, such as the following:

```
$ INITIALIZE/QUEUE/BATCH -
_$ /AUTOSTART_ON=(NODE1::, NODE2::)  SYS$BATCH
```

The INITIALIZE command only has to be performed once. This information is stored in the queue manager database. This saves time when the node is rebooted. After each boot (typically in SYS$MANAGER:SYSTARTUP_VMS.COM), the preinitialized autostart queues must be started with

```
$ ENABLE AUTOSTART/QUEUES
```

The advantage of autostart queues in a cluster environment is to provide automatic fail-over if one of the nodes becomes unavailable. In a single node environment (not a cluster), the commands would become:

```
$ INITIALIZE/QUEUE/BATCH SYS$BATCH
$ START/QUEUE SYS$BATCH
```

The initialize and autostart conventions apply to printer queues (described in the following sections) as well.

Printer Queues

Setting up a non-PostScript printer takes three steps. First, the printer is characterized by defining its capabilities (e.g., it could have an RS-232 connection, a parallel port, or a network connection). Other characteristics are also defined with the SET PRINTER command for a line printer and SET TERMINAL for a character printer. In general terms:

- The line printer, called an LPA0, is connected via the computer's parallel port.

- The spooling information is provided with the SET DEVICE command, specifically defining the spooling file's location, its name, and how it is linked to the physical device.

- The queue's characteristics are defined with the INITIALIZE command.

The following example shows how a locally connected printer (LPA0:) is defined, how it is to be spooled, and how to set up its queue (LPA0, with no colon). Incidentally, when a user prints a file, only its name and version number is recorded in the queue's database. The file is not copied; it is printed from the user's file space.

```
$ SET PRINTER/TAB/PAGE=66/WIDTH=132/LOWER/FF/NOCR -
_$ /FALLBACK/NOWRAP/NOTAB LPA0:
```

```
$ SET DEVICE/SPOOLED=(LPA0,SYS$SYSDEVICE) LPA0:

$ INITIALIZE/QUEUE/START -
_$ /DEFAULT=(NOBURST,FLAG=ALL,TRAILER=ONE) -
_$ /AUTOSTART_ON=(NODE1::LPA0:,NODE2::LPA0:)  LPA0
```

As with execution queues, subsequent boots do not require redefinition of the device or the queue. The ENABLE AUTOSTART command, which was previously described, activates the queue and makes it available for use.

The following example shows how a networked LAT[1] protocol printer is created. This process is similar to the previous example except that the connection to the print server must be defined first.

- The printer is connected to some sort of server that is serviced by LAT. Notice that a LAT Control Program (LATCP) is used first to create the "service" and then to connect to a known LAT node (HS229).

- The terminal (not the printer) is characterized with SET TERMINAL, similar to the SET PRINTER statement in the previous example.

- The queue (called LN03_1) is assigned a spooling device.

- The queue is defined.

SET TERMINAL (not SET PRINTER) is used here because the LN03 is considered a Compaq/HP terminal device.

```
$ RUN SYS$SYSTEM:LATCP
LATCP> CREATE PORT LTA3331:
LATCP> MODIFY PORT LTA3331:/NODE=HS229

$ SET TERMINAL/PAGE=100/WIDTH=200 -
_$ /DEVICE=LN03/NOBROADCAST -
_$/NOECHO/HARDCOPY/NOTYPE_AHEAD/NOFORM -
_$/NOWRAP/PASTHRU/PERMANENT LTA3331:

$ SET DEVICE/SPOOLED=(LN03_1,SYS$SYSDEVICE) LTA3331:

$ INITIALIZE /QUEUE /DEVICE=TERMINAL/ -
_$ /AUTOSTART_ON=(NODE1::LTA3331:,NODE2::LTA555:) -
_$ /RECORD_BLOCKING/BLOCK_LIMIT=600/CHARACTERISTICS=(EAST)-
_$ /SEPARATE=(NOBURST,NOTRAILER,NOFLAG,RESET=ANSI$RESET) -
_$ /DEFAULT=(NOFEED,NOBURST,FLAG=ONE,NOTRAILER,FORM=MEMO) -
_$ /LIBRARY=LN03LIBRARY /PROCESSOR=LATSYM       LN03_1
```

---

1. LAT is an acronym for Local Area Transport, a proprietary protocol invented by DEC engineers. LAT is discussed more fully in Chapter 9.

Usually, LAT printers are connected to either terminal or print servers. If so, the server must be configured as well. Different servers have different command structures so that detail is not included in this example. I assume LAT has been started when the system is booted. LAT's startup command is found in the SYSTARTUP_VMS.COM template supplied with OpenVMS.

Instead of LAT, TCP/IP can be used to communicate with the print or terminal server. This third example shows how to use TCP/IP to connect to a terminal server using TELNETSYM. First, the symbiot must be started, as illustrated. Normally, this line is included in SYSTARTUP_VMS. A single symbiot can manage up to 16 devices. If necessary, more symbiots can be started.

```
$ @SYS$STARTUP:TCPIP$TELNETSYM_STARTUP
```

To set up the queue itself, first the SET TERMINAL and SET DEVICE commands are issued, as in the previous examples, and then the INITIALIZE command is run, as follows. Notice that the addition of the /PROCESSOR and /ON qualifiers is required to define the symbiot's name and the server's TCP/IP name and port.

```
$ INITIALIZE /QUEUE /START /DEVICE=TERMINAL -
_$ /PROCESS=TCPIP$TELNETSYM -
_$ /ON="printserver1:4242"  XYZ_QUE
```

As with LAT, the printer or terminal port on the server must also be configured—a detail that is not included in this discussion.

PostScript Printing

If the printer is PostScript capable, there is an easier way to create queues. A print queue can be configured with DECprint Supervisor (DCPS) to automatically convert various file formats (e.g., ASCII text, PCL 4, ReGIS, IBM Proprinter, and Tektronix) to PostScript before transmitting them to the printer. DCPS does not support TELNETSYM (as described in the previous section) or LPD (as described in the next section) but can be used with LAT, TCP/IP, and AppleTalk networked printers and servers. DCPS supports approximately 30 Digital,[1] 25 HP, 15 Lexmark, 8 Apple, and a variety of other printers.

The steps to set up a printer with DCPS are much simpler than those outlined previously, because everything is done with a single command. The system manager must create an execution queue for each PostScript printer to be serviced. There is a template for this operation in SYS$STARTUP:DCPS$STARTUP.TEMPLATE that is used to create DCPS$STARTUP.COM. For example, to create a queue for a PostScript

---

1. The DEC printer business was sold to Genicom in the early 1990s.

printer, the following is included in DCPS$STARTUP.COM. This script would be called from SYSTARTUP_VMS when OpenVMS is booted:

```
$ @SYS$STARTUP:DCPS$EXECUTION_QUEUE -
_$ LN15$BLDG9                        - ! P1 - Execution queue name
_$ "IP_RAWTCP/16.128.144.11:3001"   - ! P2 - protocol/address
_$ DCPS_LIB  - ! P3 - Logical name for your library search list
_$ "SIDES=2" - ! P4 - Defines a default queue parameter
_$ ""        - ! P5 - Value to override/add to default qualifiers
_$ ""        - ! P6 - Communication speed
_$ ""        - ! P7 - Set device qualifier
_$ ""          ! P8 - Verify on/off
```

This operation is fully described in the *Compaq DECprint Supervisor (DCPS) for OpenVMS System Manager's Guide*. Unfortunately, this document is not available online and must be ordered from Compaq/HP. Forms and Device Control Libraries are fully supported and described in the following sections.

Management of DCPS queues uses the same commands as described in previous sections to view, hold, delete, and so on jobs in the queue and to change forms. The control library (the P3 parameter) is built as described in the following sections. Generic queues can be defined as well.

TCP/IP Printers

The UNIX-like service LPR/LPD is also available, included with the Compaq/HP TCP/IP Services product. This service is independent of the queue manager described earlier. The Line Printer Daemon (LPD) is the server that handles the incoming print request and places the file in the designated printer's queue. The Line Printer Request (LPR) is the client that is activated when a local PRINT command is issued.

The TCP/IP queues and printers are set up with an interactive command file. The resulting dialog is partially presented, as follows:

```
$ RUN SYS$SYSTEM:TCPIP$LPRSETUP[1]
TCPIP Printer Setup Program

Command < add delete view help exit >: add
Adding printer entry, type '?' for help.

Enter printer name to add : LOCAL1
Enter the FULL name of one of the following printer types:
remote local : local
Enter printer synonym:
```

---

1. For UCX users, the executable is called UCX$LPRSETUP. TCP/IP and UCX are described in Chapter 9.

```
Enter full file specification for spool directory
SPOOLER DIRECTORY 'sd' : [SYS$SPECIFIC:[TCPIP$LPD.LOCAL1]] ?
Enter full file specification for printer log file.
printer error log file 'lf' [SYS$SPECIFIC:[TCPIP$LPD]LOCAL1.LOG] ?
Enter the name of the printcap symbol you want to modify. Other
valid entry is :
    'q' to quit (no more changes)
```

This creates a UNIX-like "printcap" database called TCPIP$PRINTCAP.DAT. Once defined, the queues are started when LPD is started with the command:

```
$ @SYS$STARTUP:TCPIP$LPD_STARTUP
```

This line would normally be placed in SYSTARTUP_VMS to be executed at boot time.

Various logicals may be defined to manage LPR/LPD (e.g., to define the log file location, the manager would create TCPIP$LPD_LOGFILE; to control OpenVMS flag pages, the manager would create TCPIP$LPD_VMS_FLAGPAGES; and to control debug diagnostics, the manager would create TCPIP$LPD_DEBUG).

As in UNIX systems, Line Printer Remove (LPRM) is used to delete queue entries and Line Printer Queue (LPQ) is used to view a printer queue.

Printer Farms

The simplest print queue provides a link to a single printer. Multiple OpenVMS print queues can be connected to a single generic printer to define the root of a printer farm. A user then directs print requests to the generic queue instead of a specific printer. The generic queue directs the job to the first available printer—in effect load leveling across several printers. Generic queues are initialized as follows:

```
$ INITIALIZE/QUEUE/START/GENERIC=(HP1, HP2, HP3) HP
```

where HP1, HP2, and HP3 are previously defined queues and the new queue, HP, is the generic one. To take advantage of load leveling, the user should submit a print job such as the following example:

```
$ PRINT/QUEUE=HP MYFILE.TXT
```

The manager should create a symbol to make this task easier for the user. Something similar to the following should be in SYSLOGIN.COM (the file that runs with every login):

```
$ HPP*RINT :== PRINT/QUEUE=HP
```

Where the "*" signifies that HPP is the minimum abbreviation. Thus, the user could enter:

```
$ HPP MYFILE.TXT
```

Printer Forms

Printer forms is a mechanism for informing OpenVMS of different paper sizes and/or formats that are loaded into a printer. By creating forms, the printer symbiont knows how the margins are defined so that it starts and ends a line properly and ejects a sheet or skips over a gutter when the sheet is full.

First, the form characteristics must be defined. Multiple forms may be defined, and they are not printer-specific but logically attached to a printer later. Forms are defined once and the information kept in the queue manager's database. An example command to create a form called MEMO on 8 1/2-by-4-inch paper stock called MEMO_FORM is as follows:

```
$ DEFINE/FORM MEMO /STOCK=MEMO_FORM -
_$ /MARGIN=(TOP=2,BOTTOM=2,LEFT=6)
_$ /WIDTH=80/LENGTH=20/TRUNCATE -
_$ /DESCRIPTION="LN03 indented memo format"
```

The database of defined forms and their characteristics is displayed with the command:

```
$ SHOW QUEUE/FORM/FULL MEMO

Form name                       Number    Description
---------                       ------    -----------
MEMO (stock=MEMO   )               110    LN03 indented memo format
     /LENGTH=20 /MARGIN=(TOP=2,BOTTOM=2,LEFT=6) /STOCK=MEMO_FORM /TRUNCATE
     /WIDTH=80
```

The form can be associated with a given queue when that queue is created as shown:

```
$ INITIALIZE/QUEUE/FORM_MOUNTED=MEMO LN03_1
```

This setup is confirmed with the following command:

```
$ SHOW QUEUE/FULL LN03_1
Printer queue LN03_1, idle, on BAY::TTA3:, mounted form MEMO_FORM
  <Queue for printer in Jean's office>
  /BASE_PRIORITY=4 /DEFAULT=(FEED,FORM=MEMO (stock=MEMO_FORM))
  /OWNER=[SYSTEM]
  /PROTECTION=(S:M,O:D,G:R,W:R)
```

The way a user requests a particular form is to submit a print job similar to the following command. Notice that this command changes forms.

```
$ PRINT/FORM=MEMO/QUEUE=LN03_1 SET.TXT
```

If the queue is initialized with some other, incompatible form, however, the print job would be delayed. Thus, the PRINT command will appear in the LNO3_1 queue as follows:

```
$ SHOW ENTRY 133/FULL
Entry Jobname          Username     Blocks    Status
----- -------          --------     ------    ------
133   SET              RANDOM           74    Pending (stock type mismatch)
On idle printer queue LN03_1
Submitted 21-JAN-2000 16:14 /FORM=MEMO (stock=MEMO_FORM) /PRIORITY=100
File: _$5$DUA1:[RANDOM]SET.TXT;5
```

At this point, the operator would change the paper form in the printer and issue the following command. This would permit the job (and all others waiting for that form) to print.

```
$ SET QUEUE/FORM_MOUNTED=MEMO
```

Printer Control Libraries

Text and/or escape sequences can be inserted into the print job at three different points:

- Setup at the beginning of each file (a PRINT command can specify multiple files to be printed)

- Page setup at the beginning of each page to control font, page orientation, and so on

- Reset at the end of the job

Printer control libraries are necessary for most printers (i.e., special control sequences or PostScript must accompany most print jobs to control the printer). OpenVMS contains a default DCPS library of modules called SYS$LIBRARY:DCPS$DEVCTL.TLB, which contains printer control sequences for supported printers. Text libraries are maintained with the LIBRARY utility. The names of the modules in this library are partially displayed as follows:

```
$ libr/list dcps$devctl.tlb

Directory of TEXT library SYS$COMMON:[SYSLIB]DCPS$DEVCTL.TLB;6
on   3-SEP-2002 18:43:54
Creation date:    9-MAY-1996 05:48:30      Creator:  VAX-11 Librarian V04-00
```

```
Revision date:    9-MAY-1996 05:59:10    Library format:    3.0
Number of modules:    157                Max. key length:   39
Other entries:          0                Preallocated index blocks:    11
Recoverable deleted blocks:      0       Total index blocks used:      21
Max. Number history records:     20      Library history records:      20

DCW1000_DISPLAY
DCW1000_ENHANCED
DCW1000_HIGHRES
DCW1000_NOCORECT
DCW1000_SIMPRESS
DCW1000_STANDARD
DCW1000_VIVDBLUE
DI_BRIGHTER
```

To examine the contents of a single module within this library, first it must be
extracted with the following command:

```
$ library/extract=dcw1000_display/out=temp.txt dcps$devctl.tlb
```

Then it is displayed on the terminal with the following command. Only a portion of
this PostScript file is shown:

```
$ TYPE/PAGE TEMP.TXT

%!
%These files by Tektronix are provided for Digital Equipment Corporation
%
% Copyright (c) 1992,1993 Tektronix, Incorporated.  All rights reserved.
%
% $Revision: 1.1 $

%  Use this file to select the Simulate Display color correction.
%
%  Wrap function with startjob to make the change persistent.
%systemdict/languagelevel known{languagelevel 2 eq{true (0) startjob dup not
% {/exitserver errordict/invalidaccess get exec}if}{false}ifelse}{false}ifelse
%not {quit} if

mark
{ currentpagedevice /DeviceRenderingInfo get dup
  /Type get 2 ne
  { pop 4 dict begin /Type 2 def currentdict end } if

  begin
```

Thus, for the manager to create new modules, either this library must be modified or a
new one must be created. First, the required .TXT file is created with any editor. Then,
using LIBRARY/INSERT, that file is added to the library. If the default library is not
used, the user library is specified in the /LIBRARY= qualifier and is added to the
INITIALIZE command illustrated previously or in the DCPS command file parameter 3.

To see how a manager would perform this task, consider this example. Suppose the
printer supported landscape mode. For instance, to put the LN03 printer into
landscape requires an escape sequence, "<esc>?21 J", before the data. The manager
must perform the following steps:

- Create a new library to hold this file (or add it to an existing library).

- Create a .TXT file containing the escape sequence.

- Initialize the queue to point to this library.

- Instruct the users how to exercise the landscape option.

First, the ASCII text file (in the example LANDSCAPE.TXT) is created with any of several editors available on OpenVMS. Next, it is inserted into the library. If the library is new, it must be created first, as follows:

```
$ LIBRARY/CREATE/TEXT LN03LIBRARY.TLB
```

Once created, the file is inserted like this:

```
$ LIBRARY/INSERT LN03LIBRARY.TLB LANDSCAPE.TXT
```

Thus, the library generally contains several files, each pertaining to a different control sequence recognized by the printer. When the printer queue for the LN03 is created, the library must be specified in the /LIBRARY qualifier like this:

```
$ INITIALIZE/QUEUE/LIBRARY=LN03LIBRARY …
```

When issuing the PRINT command and including the landscape escape sequence, the following command would be issued:

```
$ PRINT/SETUP=LANDSCAPE filename
```

This PRINT command causes LANDSCAPE.TXT to be extracted from the library specified by the /LIBRARY qualifier and sends it to the printer before sending the specified file. If the print stock is landscape-oriented, it might be more convenient to include the /LIBRARY specification when declaring the form. Forms were discussed previously.

OpenVMS Management Station

Managing printer queues (but not batch or LPR/LPD queues) from Windows on a PC is done with the OpenVMS Management Station utility. The management tasks include:

- Monitoring a printer

- Examining and changing both printer and queue attributes

- Examining and changing job attributes

This utility is particularly convenient on a system with a large number of printer queues, because of the compact visual presentation. The Management Station can also be used to manage disks and accounts.

Summary

- The queue manager (QUEMAN) is required for execution (batch) or print queues, except for the UNIX-like LPR/LPD print queues. It is started with START/QUEUE/MANAGER.

- The queue manager database is located with the logical QMAN$MASTER.

- Print and batch queues are created with the INITIALIZE/QUEUE command.

- Queues may be autostarted (in case of node failure) or started explicitly.

- Print queues normally need additional information to characterize the printer. This is defined with SET TERMINAL, SET PRINTER, and SET DEVICE commands.

- Printer farms are headed with generic queues.

- Printer forms can be created to define specific paper characteristics (e.g., width, length) and to help the operator manage which physical forms are mounted in a specific printer.

- Printer control libraries can be created to automatically send text and escape sequences before and/or after each job is printed. This ensures that the printer is properly configured to print the specific file.

- Queues for PostScript printers are treated differently, and files can be automatically converted to PostScript format for printing.

- UNIX-like LPR/LPD is also supported by OpenVMS.

Related Publications

1. The *OpenVMS System Manager's Manual*, Chapter 13, discusses the queue manager, and Chapter 14 discusses queues.

2. The specific queuing commands are defined in the *OpenVMS DCL Dictionary*.

3. TCP/IP network printers are discussed in *Compaq TCP/IP Services for OpenVMS Management*, Part 6, for TCP/IP printers. See LATCP *OpenVMS System Management Utilities Reference Manual*, Chapter 13, if the printer uses LAT protocol.

4. The *OpenVMS Management Station Overview and Release Notes* is only a brief description. Full documentation is available once the program is installed on the PC under the HELP feature.

5. The *Compaq DECprint Supervisor (DCPS) for OpenVMS* is not currently available online. This product is licensed with the OpenVMS license.

6. The *OpenVMS Command Definition, Librarian, and Message Utilities Manual* details the use of the LIBRARY command.

Chapter 6 — Backup

OpenVMS has the capability to:

- Back up and restore individual files, directory structures, and whole disks, including the system disk (complete with boot records).

- Back up and then immediately verify the results against the original files.

- Incrementally back up files that changed or are new since the last full backup.

- List file names in the backup container (called a *save set*).

- Support disk-to-disk, disk-to-tape, and tape-to-disk backup and restore operations.

- Support disk-to-disk copy operations.

- Perform all of these operations on shadowed disks.

- Use the Save Set Manager (SSMgr) to keep track of backup save sets.

Unlike UNIX, one disk backup program, BACKUP, is available in OpenVMS. The BACKUP program will perform disk copy, disk backup, and disk restore functions. The backup destination can be either another disk or tape. BACKUP will support other media as well, but only tape and disks are practical because of their capacity. For instance, a CD or DVD could be used as backup media. An entire disk can be copied, a subdirectory tree and files, or only those files that changed since the last backup can be saved. This latter operation is called *incremental backup*. The backed-up data is not compressed, but, depending on the device and BACKUP options, a BACKUP-generated checksum in the form of a cyclic redundancy check (CRC) accompanies the data files to aid in media error recovery. Active CRC is the default, but it can be turned off with the /NOCRC qualifier. Most modern tape drives operate in compression mode and/or CRC mode by default. Permitting BACKUP to compute the CRC as well is like having both suspenders and a belt to hold up your pants.

Image Backup

An *image backup* is one that copies an entire disk, not selected files or directory trees, to another device. If the backup is performed on a system disk, the necessary boot records are copied as well. This is also called a *full backup*. If the destination is a tape, everything on disk is written to a container file on tape. This container file is termed a *save set*. The commands for this operation are as follows:

```
$ BACKUP/IMAGE/VERIFY/RECORD/IGNORE=INTERLOCK -
_$ DUA0: -
_$ MUA400:FULLBU.SAV/REWIND/LABEL=FULL
```

Reading the BACKUP command line from left to right, it specifies that an image backup is to be created.

- The /IMAGE qualifier signifies the option.

- The /VERIFY qualifier specifies that after the tape is written, all files in the save set are to be read back and compared to the original on disk.

- The /RECORD qualifier causes BACKUP to add the date and time of the backup operation to each file on disk. This provides an audit trail for the manager and is used for incremental backups, as described later. The date is accessed as shown:

```
$ dir/date=backup login.com;0

Directory FACULTY:[DMILLER]

LOGIN.COM;101         24-AUG-2002 07:51:35.60
```

- If the disk is mounted so that anyone may access it, open files will not be backed up. To avoid this treatment, add the /IGNORE=INTERLOCK qualifier.

- The source is a disk on device DUA0:.

- The destination is a tape on device MUA400:.

- The save set is to be named FULLBU.SAV.

- The /REWIND qualifier ensures that the tape will be initialized before backup.

- The /LABEL qualifier specifies the logical label assigned to the tape and is limited to six characters.

If the tape is too small to contain all of the files on the disk, the operator will be instructed to supply a new tape. When he or she responds to the prompt, the backup operation continues. The dialog is similar to the following:

```
%BACKUP-I-RESUME, resuming operation on volume 2
%BACKUP-I-READYWRITE, mount volume FULL on MUA400: for writing
Respond with YES when ready:
```

Alternately, tape robots can be connected to the tape drive to switch tapes automatically.

If the destination is another disk, there is another option. The destination disk can contain either a save set or a directory tree. This latter option is termed a *disk-to-disk copy*. The command is illustrated as follows. The destination disk, DUA300:, has to be private, not public, because it will be completely reinitialized and it should be large enough to contain all of the files on DUA0:. This is not a bit-by-bit copy, and DUA300: will be a defragmented version of DUA0:.

If defragmentation is the goal, Disk File Optimizer (DFO), Compaq/HP's defragmention program, will run on an active disk to defragment both files and free space.

```
$ BACKUP/IMAGE/VERIFY/RECORD/IGNORE=INTERLOCK -
_$ DUA0: -
_$ DUA300:
```

Thus, DUA300: becomes an exact duplicate of DUA0:. If DUA0: is bootable, DUA300: will be as well.

Image Restore

Restoring a disk (i.e., an image) from tape is easily done by reversing the backup command; however, the disk must be private, because it will be completely overwritten. The command is:

```
$ BACKUP/IMAGE/VERIFY -
_$ MUA400:FULLBU.SAV/REWIND/LABEL=FULL -
_$ DUA0:
```

Selected files and/or directories can be restored from an image backup, too. For instance, to restore all files in the [REPORTS] directory tree from tape back to disk, the following command would be used:

```
$ BACKUP/IMAGE/VERIFY -
_$ MUA400:FULLBU.SAV/REWIND/LABEL=FULL/SELECT=[REPORTS...]  -
_$ DUA0:[REPORTS...]
```

Incremental Backup

After an image backup of the disk is made, incremental backups can be performed periodically. An incremental backup contains only the files created since the image backup. The backup date associated with each file is examined to determine if it is newly created. Incremental backups are usually smaller (because fewer files are involved) and therefore are performed faster than an image backup. There is no concept of UNIX backup levels in OpenVMS.

Two types of incremental backups are supported: cumulative and differential. A *cumulative backup* includes all changes since the image backup and is performed with this command:

```
$ BACKUP/VERIFY/IGNORE=INTERLOCK -
_$ DUA0:[000000...]*.*;*/SINCE=BACKUP -
_$ MUA400:CUM.SAV/REWIND/LABEL=CUMULA
```

This command states (on the second line) that all of DUA0: is to be searched for files created since the last full backup. Only those files are copied to MUA400:. Every time the cumulative backup runs, the save set grows, because the number of files created since the last image backup undoubtedly increases.

The *differential backup* command is similar; only one qualifier is added to the first line. The /RECORD specifies that the backup date of those files that are backed up are to be recorded so they are not backed up again. Hence, the command changes to this:

```
$ BACKUP/VERIFY/RECORD/IGNORE=INTERLOCK -
_$ DUA0:[000000...]*.*;*/SINCE=BACKUP -
_$ MUA400:DIFF.SAV/REWIND/LABEL=DIFFER
```

Successive differential backups only capture files created since the last differential backup, and the save set size is relatively constant each time it is run.

Incremental Restore

Only the latest image backup and the latest cumulative backup tape are used in the restore operation. The destination disk will be completely overwritten in this process. The image backup tape is restored to disk first. This is the same operation as shown previously. Then the latest cumulative backup tape is restored. That command is similar to the following:

```
$ BACKUP/INCREMENTAL/VERIFY -
_$ MUA400:CUM.SAV/REWIND/LABEL=CUMULA -
_$ DUA0:
```

If restoring differential save sets, as similar command is repeated for each tape, starting with the most recent.

To compare the various backup methods, consider both the backup and the restore operations. A differential backup is the smallest and therefore takes the least amount of time to perform. The cumulative backup is sort of a sum of differential backups. It is larger than a differential backup and takes longer to produce. The image backup is the largest and takes the most time to generate.

An image backup is the fastest to restore because only one save set is required. If cumulative backups are performed, first the image backup is restored and then the latest cumulative backup is restored. If differential backups are performed, first the image backup is restored and then the latest differential backup is restored, then the one previous to that, and so forth until all differential backups are restored. This latter option obviously takes the most amount of time. Thus, the system manager must trade off backup time and restore time when deciding a backup strategy.

Backup with Volume Shadowing

Volume shadowing binds one, two, or three physical disks together logically in a shadow set. When a write takes place to one disk in the shadow set, that data is forwarded to all members of the set to ensure data integrity. This is not the same as a backup operation for various reasons. For instance, it does not protect against accidental file deletion or software failures.

The shadow set can be backed up and restored using BACKUP with additional care. To see how this is done, consider the following commands. At boot time, assume the shadow set, DSA1:, is formed with three member disks, as shown:

```
$ MOUNT/SYSTEM DSA1:/SHADOW=($1$DUA8:, $1$DUA9:, $1$DUA10:) USER
```

At some time later, the manager decides to back up this shadow set. This is done by using the shadow set name, not one of the member's names.

```
$ BACKUP/IMAGE/VERIFY/RECORD/IGNORE=INTERLOCK -
_$ DSA1: -
_$ MUA400:FULLBU.SAV/REWIND/LABEL=FULL
```

This method has the usual cautions regarding open files described previously. If the manager wants to back up the shadow set without worrying about these restrictions, the shadow set has to be manipulated. One of its members must be removed first. First, the shadow set has to be dissolved.

```
$ DISMOUNT/SYSTEM DSA1:
```

Next, it is remounted with one of the members removed.

```
$ MOUNT/SYSTEM DSA1:/SHADOW=($1$DUA8:, $1$DUA9:) USER
```

Now that removed member can be backed up without worrying about open files:

```
$ BACKUP/IMAGE/VERIFY/RECORD -
_$ $1$DUA10: -
_$ MUA400:FULLBU.SAV/REWIND/LABEL=FULL
```

After the backup is complete, this disk can rejoin the shadow set. Any changes that have taken place to the shadow set during the backup period will be made to 1DUA10 when it joins.

```
$ MOUNT DSA1:/SHADOW=$1$DUA10:
```

Restore with Volume Shadowing

Whenever rebuilding a disk from an image backup, the disk is unavailable for other uses. The volume shadow restore operation requires that the shadow set be dissolved before the restore operation. After the restoration is complete, the shadow set is reformed with the newly restored disk as the base. As the other disks are added, they are made to match this restored disk. In the following example, assume the same shadow set as before is used. First, dissolve the shadow set:

```
$ DISMOUNT/SYSTEM DSA1:
```

Next, restore the save set to one of the devices like this. The MOUNT/FOREIGN command has been left out of previous examples to simplify them. Because this example is a bit more complicated, that command is illustrated as well.

```
$ MOUNT/FOREIGN/OVERRIDE=SHADOW $1$DUA8:

$ BACKUP/IMAGE/VERIFY -
_$ MUA400:FULLBU.SAV/REWIND/LABEL=FULL -
_$ $1$DUA8:
```

Finally, recreate the shadow set based on the newly restored 1DUA8:. Let OpenVMS (or the RAID controller) take care of synchronizing the other disks.

```
$ MOUNT/SYSTEM DSA1:/SHADOW=($1$DUA8:, $1$DUA9:, $1$DUA10:) USER
```

If incremental backups are involved, they would be applied before recreating the shadow set just as in the restore examples. This case will not be discussed further.

Summary

Other BACKUP options and capabilities were not discussed. The points that were made are:

- BACKUP is the only comprehensive tool program available. It is used to both back up and restore files.

- Several backup options are available, including image or full backup, cumulative incremental backup, and differential incremental backup.

- When a backup is performed, the files are normally stored in a save set or container file.

- BACKUP will also copy directory trees from disk to disk or from one directory on disk to another.

- Shadow sets can be backed up and restored if the manager follows certain procedures.

Related Publications

1. The *OpenVMS System Manager's Manual*, Chapter 11, discusses the several BACKUP options in detail with examples and scenarios.

2. The BACKUP command is formally described in the *OpenVMS System Management Utilities Reference Manual,* although the *Manager's Manual's* examples are much more extensive.

3. Backing up a shadow set is discussed in *Volume Shadowing for OpenVMS.*

Chapter 7 — System Monitoring and Performance Management

OpenVMS has the capability to:

- Examine hardware status reports.

- Monitor CPU, disk, and memory performance either locally or across the cluster.

- Monitor file system performance.

- Monitor network performance.

- Monitor hardware errors.

- Automatically or manually adjust system parameters to change performance.

- Tune OpenVMS according to the physical resources it supports.

The system manager is responsible for monitoring the system operation. This includes monitoring the hardware for error reports and optimizing hardware and software resources for the average workload. These tasks should be carried out periodically, and long-term statistics must be maintained so that changes from the norm can be quickly identified and isolated. Waiting until the system is performing badly to collect this data is not effective management.

Monitor Hardware Status

If a hardware component detects an error, it is reported by OpenVMS. Information about the failure, whether it is recoverable or not, is recorded in SYS$ERRORLOG:ERRLOG.SYS. The primary command for examining this log file is SHOW ERROR, and its use in a cluster environment is as follows:

```
$ mcr sysman
SYSMAN> set environment/cluster

command environment:
        Clusterwide on local cluster
        Username SYSTEM        will be used on nonlocal nodes

SYSMAN> do show error
command execution on node BEAVER
Device                          Error Count
PEA0:                               3
```

```
command execution on node LOON
Device                          Error Count
PEA0:                                2
command execution on node CSWWW
Device                          Error Count
PEA0:                                2
command execution on node EAGLE
%SHOW-S-NOERRORS, no device errors found
```

The previous report shows errors on the cluster communications device, PEA0. Clusters are discussed in Chapter 10.

SHOW ERROR displays a summary of hardware errors and thus alerts the manager to possible hardware failures. It is important to monitor all errors, because hardware usually does not fail catastrophically without warning; rather minor problems are encountered before total failure. So, if an error is observed in the SHOW ERROR display, the manager should use additional programs and commands to investigate the error further.

Device and CPU errors are examined with DIAGNOSE (on OpenVMS/Alpha) and ANALYZE/ERROR. An illustration of the latter command is as follows. As shown elsewhere in other commands, reporting levels are generally available. Commonly / BRIEF (or /SUMMARY) displays the least amount of information.

```
$ ANALYZE/ERROR/BRIEF

Error Log Report Generator                              Version V7.1
****************************** ENTRY    1. ******************************
ERROR SEQUENCE 0.                           LOGGED ON:      SID 13002602
DATE/TIME 16-SEP-2002 00:05:35.93                      SYS_TYPE 04130002
SYSTEM UPTIME: 11 DAYS 14:23:12
SCS NODE: BEAVER                                            VAX/VMS V7.1

ERRLOG.SYS CREATED KA49  CPU Microcode Rev # 2.  CONSOLE FW REV# 1.3
                   Standard Microcode Patch    Patch Rev # 19.
****************************** ENTRY    2. ******************************
ERROR SEQUENCE 2343.                        LOGGED ON:      SID 13002602
DATE/TIME 16-SEP-2002 22:55:36.05                      SYS_TYPE 04130002
SYSTEM UPTIME: 12 DAYS 13:12:45
SCS NODE: BEAVER                                            VAX/VMS V7.1

TIME STAMP KA49  CPU Microcode Rev # 2.  CONSOLE FW REV# 1.3
                   Standard Microcode Patch    Patch Rev # 19.
****************************** ENTRY    3. ******************************
ERROR SEQUENCE 2344.                        LOGGED ON:      SID 13002602
DATE/TIME 16-SEP-2002 22:57:12.85                      SYS_TYPE 04130002
SYSTEM UPTIME: 12 DAYS 13:14:22
SCS NODE: BEAVER                                            VAX/VMS V7.1

ERL$LOGMESSAGE KA49  CPU Microcode Rev # 2.  CONSOLE FW REV# 1.3
                   Standard Microcode Patch    Patch Rev # 19.

NI-SCS SUB-SYSTEM, _BEAVER$PEA0:

    PORT HAS CLOSED VIRTUAL CIRCUIT

****************************** ENTRY    4. ******************************
ERROR SEQUENCE 2350.                        LOGGED ON:      SID 13002602
```

```
DATE/TIME 16-SEP-2002 23:55:36.05                    SYS_TYPE 04130002
SYSTEM UPTIME: 12 DAYS 14:12:45
SCS NODE: BEAVER                                      VAX/VMS V7.1

TIME STAMP KA49  CPU Microcode Rev # 2.  CONSOLE FW REV# 1.3
                 Standard Microcode Patch    Patch Rev # 19.
```

In my system, the ERRLOG.SYS is reinitialized every day to keep its size manageable. Entries 1, 2, and 4 in the previous display pertain to stopping and restarting the error logger at midnight and identifying the hardware. Entry 3 relates to the PEA0 error. More data about that error is available but not presented here.

In my experience, memory problems start with correctable errors that later may become permanent. In the case of memory errors, OpenVMS will automatically stop using memory pages that have reported errors during the boot memory scan. SHOW MEMORY is the primary program used to examine memory status, although ANALYZE/ERROR can also be used. SHOW MEMORY is illustrated as follows:

```
$ SHOW MEMORY

              System Memory Resources on 21-SEP-2002 18:51:31.05

Physical Memory Usage (pages):     Total      Free     In Use    Modified
    Main Memory (256.00Mb)         32768     28089       4357         322

Virtual I/O Cache (Kbytes):        Total      Free     In Use
    Cache Memory                    3200        16       3184

Granularity Hint Regions (pages):  Total      Free     In Use    Released
    Execlet code region              512         0        506           6
    Execlet data region               96         4         92           0
    S0/S1 Executive data region      477         0        477           0
    S2 Executive data region         160         0        160           0
    Resident image code region       512         0        319         193

Slot Usage (slots):                Total      Free    Resident     Swapped
    Process Entry Slots               35        15         20           0
    Balance Set Slots                 33        15         18           0

Dynamic Memory Usage (bytes):      Total      Free     In Use     Largest
    Nonpaged Dynamic Memory      4243456    373824    3869632        5952
    Paged Dynamic Memory         4661248   1119936    3541312     1069792

Buffer Object Usage (pages):                In Use       Peak
    32-bit System Space Windows (S0/S1)          0          0
    64-bit System Space Windows (S2)             0          0

Memory Reservations (pages):              Reserved     In Use        Type
Total (0 Mb reserved)                            0          0

Paging File Usage (blocks):                   Free Reservable       Total
    DISK$ALPHASYS:[SYS0.SYSEXE]SWAPFILE.SYS     4480       4480        4480
    DISK$ALPHASYS:[SYS0.SYSEXE]PAGEFILE.SYS   532480     479472      532480


Of the physical pages in use, 2847 pages are permanently allocated to OpenVMS.
```

This command presents a plethora of statistics about various aspects of how the memory is used. This data can be used for performance tuning, described later. It will also include error reports, if there are any.

Application Software Errors

Another source of problems may be related to poorly programmed applications or errors on the part of inexperienced users. Problems such as program looping, page thrashing, and excessive I/O can be isolated to a process with the SHOW SYSTEM command (akin to the UNIX ps command) as shown, in part, as follows:

```
$ show system

OpenVMS V7.1  on node BEAVER  22-SEP-2002 14:45:26.41  Uptime  18 05:02:35
  Pid    Process Name    State  Pri    I/O      CPU        Page flts  Pages
20200081 SWAPPER          HIB    16      0   0 00:00:04.68       0       0
20200086 CONFIGURE        HIB    10     39   0 00:00:00.04     174     242
20200088 IPCACP           HIB    10      7   0 00:00:00.01      96     175
20200089 ERRFMT           HIB     7  11746   0 00:00:21.90     147     232
2020008A CACHE_SERVER     HIB    16    994   0 00:00:00.44      80     129
2020008B CLUSTER_SERVER   HIB     8    324   0 00:00:03.14     328     557
2020008C OPCOM            HIB     8   4605   0 00:00:05.90    1288     228
2020008D AUDIT_SERVER     HIB    10   1639   0 00:00:03.18     682    1030
2020008E JOB_CONTROL      HIB    10   2565   0 00:00:04.68     277     417
2020008F QUEUE_MANAGER    HIB     8  34875   0 00:02:42.98    1400    1802
20200090 SECURITY_SERVER  HIB    10   1354   0 00:00:07.37    1915    1516
20200091 SMISERVER        HIB     9    147   0 00:00:00.42     666     725
20200092 NETACP           HIB    10  36980   0 00:00:06.91     216     436
20200093 EVL              HIB     6    237   0 00:00:00.21     510     482 N
20200094 REMACP           HIB     8    183   0 00:00:00.12     108      78
20200095 LATACP           HIB    14     63   0 00:00:23.92     326     296
20200096 LANACP           HIB    13     37   0 00:00:00.10     431     652
20200097 UCX$INET_ACP     HIB     8   2671   0 00:00:07.73     455     481
20200098 UCX$INET_ROUTED  LEF     6     37   0 00:00:00.13     395     623 S
20200099 IUPOP3 Server    HIB     6   3859   0 00:00:08.91    7923    1359
202000A7 DECW$SERVER_0    HIB     6    546   0 00:00:01.73    3479    1073
202000A8 MSAF$SERVER0     COM     4    362   0 00:00:01.02    1530     172
202000A9 DECW$LOGINOUT    LEF     4    152   0 00:00:00.92    4068    2470
202000AA MSAP$RCVR0       HIB     6     37   0 00:00:00.12     962     718
20200D39 SYSTEM           CUR     4    206   0 00:00:00.55    1618     383
```

Furthermore, details about a specific process are available using SHOW PROCESS/ ID=. Various levels of detail are available using additional qualifiers. The following example shows only basic information:

```
$ show process/id=20200d39

22-SEP-2002 14:48:21.24    User: SYSTEM          Process ID:    20200D39
                           Node: BEAVER          Process name:  "SYSTEM"

Terminal:
  TNA384:  (Host: 94.phoenix-12rh16rt-az.dial-access.att.net Port: 1086 )
User Identifier:    [SYSTEM]
Base priority:      4
Default file spec:  SYS$COMMON:[SYSMGR]

Devices allocated:  BEAVER$TNA384:
```

Thus, the use of SHOW SYSTEM and SHOW PROCESS gives the manager detailed information about any process running on the system. This information can be used to isolate software errors, to tune the particular process, or even to tune the system.

Introduction to Performance Management

Performance management of a specific process or of the entire system largely depends on the manager's common sense. The resource (i.e., the computer system) is finite, and performance improvements cannot be squeezed out of it indefinitely. Before embarking on any system improvements, a plan must be carefully developed. Key elements of that plan include the following:

- Measure and characterize the average system performance as it exists before any changes.

- Based on step 1, identify a single bottleneck. It is important to attack only one problem at a time to eliminate unintended interactions between multiple changes. Quantify the improvement you expect to see (e.g., a goal might be stated as "reduce I/Os per second by 10 percent").

- Investigate that single bottleneck to determine how best to attain the improvement goal.

- Implement that change. Record everything that is done so the change can be backed out if necessary.

- Repeat exactly the measurements taken in step 1 and examine the bottleneck identified in step 2 again. Determine if the goal was attained. Also, make sure the change did not adversely affect any other measurement.

- If the bottleneck improvement goal was not reached, back out the change and start again at step 3 to find another approach.

- If the bottleneck goal was reached, you may want to repeat the entire process, concentrating on another bottleneck, and create a new goal.

Generally, tuning OpenVMS is unnecessary and should be considered only as a last resort, because running AUTOGEN regularly (discussed in the next section) should identify and correct normal retuning activities. Assuming the manager uses AUTOGEN and considers its suggested changes, several other options should be considered before changing OpenVMS parameters. Some possibilities are:

- Restrict the number of interactive logins.

- Reduce the priority of resource-intensive interactive programs.

- Move resource-intensive programs to the batch stream or run them at night or on weekends.

- INSTALL programs that are used often. This will reduce disk I/O.

- Move certain system files off the system disk to reduce system disk contention.

- Likewise, scatter often-accessed user disk files over several disks.

- Stripe heavily used disks to improve I/O throughput.

An OpenVMS manager-novice should be warned that without a thorough understanding of the OpenVMS parameters and without a complete understanding of the OpenVMS algorithms depending on those parameters, changes may do more harm than good. For instance, the OpenVMS paging algorithm is complex and involves several parameters. If a process is thrashing (thus causing excessive page faults), modifying the process, not OpenVMS, is the recommended approach. For instance, the process might be recoded or its quotas could be increased; however, the Compaq/HP and third-party tuning manuals describe the paging algorithm in great detail, explaining the purpose of each of the parameters. So the manager can knowledgeably tune the algorithm if necessary.

The resources that can be monitored and tuned in OpenVMS are:

- CPU

- Memory

- Disk I/O

- Several network protocol I/Os

The first step to effect performance management is to establish average peak workload baseline measurements on the system as it is currently configured. The baseline data is collected at the busiest time of day, or perhaps the busiest time of the week or month depending on your business's computer needs.

There are many possible approaches to resolving performance issues. It is important for the manager to understand the difference between workload and system capacity. Depending on the characteristics of the jobs running on the computer, there may be several possible solutions. The *OpenVMS Performance Management Manual* includes detailed algorithms used to identify and correct performance issues.

Several programs can be used to investigate system performance that may lead to either a hardware or software modification. This section introduces only two of the most commonly used performance measurement programs. Compaq/HP recommends that even if you are not having performance problems, you should record key performance measures to establish a baseline for future investigations.

For instance, MONITOR (described later) has an option (/RECORD) to save results in a file.

The other programs that are available in OpenVMS are:

- Accounting utility (ACCOUNTING)

- Audit analysis utility (ANALYZE/AUDIT)

- Authorize utility (RUN AUTHORIZE)

- Various SHOW commands

- Compaq/HP availability manager (also called DECamds)

- DECevent utility (on Alpha platforms)

- Error log utility (ANALYZE/ERROR_LOG) on VAX platforms

AUTOGEN Performance Monitoring

The primary tuning program is automated in a script called SYS$UPDATE:AUTOGEN. It is fully described in the *OpenVMS System Manager's Manual* and the *OpenVMS System Management Utilities Reference Manual*. AUTOGEN is run automatically when OpenVMS is installed or upgraded, and nearly 100 system parameters are affected. This is necessary to optimize the various system tables and buffer sizes to the specific hardware configuration. The resulting system is tuned to the hardware but not to the user load. The system manager should manually run AUTOGEN in the feedback mode whenever the system hardware or software changes or when the workload changes.

The second use of AUTOGEN is to adjust for performance under load. Compaq/HP recommends that the AUTOGEN feedback option (which gathers performance data but makes no changes) be used weekly to monitor OpenVMS performance under actual running conditions. When run this way, key performance data gathered continuously by OpenVMS can be analyzed by AUTOGEN, which then recommends changes via a report. The report should be analyzed by the manager, who determines whether the system parameters should be changed. AUTOGEN can modify about 25 key system parameters based on peak system load.

Feedback data is collected with the command, and information is stored in SYS$SYSTEM:AGEN$FEEDBACK.DAT. It will be processed at a later time.

```
$ @SYS$UPDATE:AUTOGEN SAVPARAMS SAVPARAMS FEEDBACK
```

Later, when it is convenient, the system manager runs AUTOGEN again using that previously collected feedback data to determine possible changes to OpenVMS parameters. This is done with the following command:

```
$ @SYS$UPDATE:AUTOGEN GETDATA TESTFILES FEEDBACK
```

AUTOGEN then reports what the new parameter values should be in a file called SYS$SYSTEM:AGEN$PARAMS.REPORT. The report resembles the following:

```
SYS$SYSTEM? type agen$params.report
AUTOGEN Parameter Calculation Report on node: BEAVER
  This information was generated at 26-AUG-2002 10:45:31.75
  AUTOGEN was run from GETDATA to TESTFILES using FEEDBACK

** No changes will be done by AUTOGEN **
  The values given in this report are what AUTOGEN would
   have set the parameters to.


Processing Parameter Data files
-------------------------------

Including parameters from: SYS$SYSTEM:MODPARAMS.DAT

Including parameters from:  SYS$MANAGER:AGEN$NEW_NODE_DEFAULTS.DAT

Feedback information was collected on 26-AUG-2002 00:05:25.03
  Old values below are the parameter values at the time of collection.
  The feedback data is based on 499 hours of up time.
  Feedback information will be used in the subsequent calculations


Parameter information follows:
-------------------------------

MAXPROCESSCNT parameter information:
        Feedback information.
            Old value was 110, New value is 90
            Maximum Observed Processes: 46

GBLPAGFIL parameter information:
        Override Information - parameter calculation has been overridden.
            The calculated value was 1024.  The new value is 51024.
            GBLPAGFIL has been increased by 50000.
            GBLPAGFIL is not allowed to be less than 10000.

GBLPAGES parameter information:
        Feedback information.
            Old value was 156354, New value is 496878
            Peak used GBLPAGES: 65456
            Global buffer requirements: 51024
        Override Information - parameter calculation has been overridden.
            The calculated value was 129600.  The new value is 496878.
            GBLPAGES has been increased by 367278.
            GBLPAGES is not allowed to be less than 62000.
```

Once the manager reviews the changes and deems them necessary, AUTOGEN is run a third time (using the same feedback data) to make the changes to xVMSSYS.PAR.[1] This necessarily involves rebooting the system, and the command is:

```
$ @SYS$UPDATE:AUTOGEN GETDATA REBOOT FEEDBACK
```

Automated feedback data collection should be done daily and tuning perhaps weekly or whenever the system load changes. Because tuning (not feedback collection or analysis) requires rebooting, the system manager will have to carefully schedule this operation. AUTOGEN adjusts variables (some are interdependent) that control CPU, memory, and I/O performance. This data is stored in xVMSSYS.PAR so it is not lost after a boot. This file acts like the Windows NT Registry.

Manual tuning is done using the SYSMAN PARAMETER command, but a novice to OpenVMS internals should not attempt this task, because several hundred variables in xVMSSYS.PAR are quite complicated, and many of them depend on one another. Rather than using SYSMAN, the best management policy is to enter changes in MODPARAMS.DAT so AUTOGEN respects them when it runs. Thus, MODPARAMS.DAT serves as a documented history of changes to system parameters.

Variables other than those that control OpenVMS performance are stored in xVMSSYS.PAR. For instance, seven variables control login characteristics, such as how many unsuccessful login attempts are permitted, how long to inhibit login to an account after unsuccessful login, and the minimum number of characters in a password. SYSGEN PARAMETER is used to change this class of parameters. This topic is further discussed in Chapter 8.

Real-time Performance Monitoring

Once AUTOGEN has adjusted the basic system parameters, other programs can be applied if the manager believes there are performance problems. These include the following:

- Examining the error log for hardware problems, discussed earlier

- Using DECevent to determine if unusual events are occuring

- Examining system performance statistics via MONITOR and the particular TCP/IP stack the manager has installed

- If DECnet or TCPIP is used, examining network performance statistics

- Tracking other resources with accounting, such as printer usage

---

1. Actually VAXVMSSYS.PAR on VAX machines and ALPHAVMSSYS.PAR on Alpha machines.

- Using SHOW CLUSTER to track cluster resources

System performance can be monitored in real time or recorded for future analysis by the MONITOR program. This task is described in the *OpenVMS System Management Utilities Reference Manual*. This utility has about 20 suboptions, and data can be presented in a graphic-like display (the first example that follows) or a tabular display (as in the second example).

- MONITOR SYSTEM summarizes several of the other options. The display looks like this and is updated every six seconds:

```
Node: NODE1           OpenVMS Monitor Utility      12-FEB-2002 12:44:32
Statistic: CURRENT         SYSTEM STATISTICS
                                                     Process States
        + CPU Busy (100)          -+      LEF:   25      LEFO:    0
        |*************************|        HIB:   11      HIBO:    0
CPU   0 +-------------------------+ 100    COM:    8      COMO:    0
        |*                        |        PFW:    0      Other:   0
        +-------------------------+        MWAIT:  0
        Cur Top: BATCH_77 (6)                      Total: 44

        + Page Fault Rate (1468)   -    + Free List Size (35173)   +
        |****|********************|     |***************          | 54K
MEM   0 +------------------------+500   +-------------------------+
        |****                    |      |************             | 5765
        +------------------------+      + Mod List Size (3078)    +
        Cur Top: BATCH_29 (78)

        + Direct I/O Rate (412)    -+   + Buffered I/O Rate (110) -+
        |*********************     |    |*****                    |
I/O   0 +------------------------+500   +-------------------------+ 500
        |*                        |     |                         |
        +------------------------+      +-------------------------+
        Cur Top: BATCH_77 (23)         Cur Top: BATCH_77 (6)
```

- MONITOR IO /ALL produces a display similar to the following. I/O on a specific device can also be monitored.

```
              OpenVMS Monitor Utility
               I/O SYSTEM STATISTICS
                  on node NODE1
               10-FEB-2002 22:12:44
```

	CUR	AVE	MIN	MAX
Direct I/O Rate	14.33	4.46	0.33	15.33
Buffered I/O Rate	20.91	47.47	24.91	69.00
Mailbox Write Rate	0.00	0.45	0.00	2.95
Split Transfer Rate	1.66	1.56	0.33	3.97
File Open Rate	1.66	1.26	0.33	2.98
Page Fault Rate	20.58	52.31	17.33	178.00
Page Read Rate	14.29	9.00	0.00	26.88
Page Read I/O Rate	2.65	2.43	0.00	6.22

```
Page Write Rate        0.00     6.69     0.00     58.66
Page Write I/O Rate    0.00     0.27     0.00      1.66
Inswap Rate            0.00     0.00     0.00      0.00
Free List Size      3691.00  3604.09  3392.00   3771.00
Modified List Size   149.00    73.36     4.00    181.00
```

No attempt is made to explain these displays, only to illustrate the number and variety of categories and presentation methods. The Compaq/HP documents explain these categories very well.

I have spent some time describing various algorithms and data structures used by OpenVMS in my book *OpenVMS Operating System Concepts*. The point is that from these displays (and others like them), an observer can focus on the resources that are overtaxed. Once the problem resource is identified, various solutions can be proposed, implemented, tested, and compared.

Summary

- SHOW ERROR is useful to quickly ascertain hardware health.

- ANALYZE/ERROR is used to delve into the specifics of a given device error.

- AUTOGEN is run automatically when OpenVMS is installed or upgraded to adjust system parameters to the hardware configuration.

- AUTOGEN should be run periodically to capture data that OpenVMS collects. Thius data reflects actual loading.

- Certain system parameters are not touched by AUTOGEN and must be manually adjusted to reflect site policy and usage.

- MONITOR is used to examine performance in real time and in background.

- Several other performance programs are provided by Compaq/HP for tuning and planning purposes.

References

1. The Compaq/HP document dedicated to system performance is called *OpenVMS Performance Management*. This book describes the tuning algorithm extensively. It also describes how to use the performance programs available with OpenVMS.

2. Monitoring and tuning TCP/IP are described in *Compaq TCP/IP Services for OpenVMS Tuning and Troubleshooting*.

3. The *Compaq Availability Manager User's Guide* is at. It can be run from either an OpenVMS terminal or a Windows terminal.

4. DECevent is described in the *OpenVMS System Management Utilities Reference Manual*.

5. The *OpenVMS System Manager's Manual*, Chapter 15, discusses AUTOGEN usage in detail. The *OpenVMS System Management Utilities Reference Manual* details its options.

6. My book, *OpenVMS Operating System Concepts*, describes paging and thrashing in great detail.

7. Coburn, James W. *OpenVMS Performance Management*, second edition. This book addresses specific algorithms used to test and adjust OpenVMS. Because it is dated, this text should be used in conjunction with *OpenVMS Performance Management*.

Chapter 8 — Security

OpenVMS has the capability to:

- Manage account passwords and other account parameters.

- Monitor and control account intrusions (break-ins).

- Maintain a password history.

- Group users into security classes.

- Place access restrictions on system resources: disks, files, queues.

- Control access to restricted programs.

- Keep logs of errors, break-in attempts, file accesses, operator actions, and so on.

OpenVMS's out-of-the-box default security level is C2, as defined by the U.S. Computer Security Center's *Orange Book*. OpenVMS 6.1 is the most recent version formally accepted as C2 compliant. OpenVMS is also available as a B1 level.

The system manager has the responsibility to tailor his or her system for the specific environment. More often than not, I have used Department of Defense "secured" systems that were wide open to the authorized users (i.e., everyone was granted unlimited privileges). Granted, the machine and the network it was connected to were behind a security door with limited access, but the manager made no effort to protect the users from one another or from the applications running on that machine. Certainly, no malicious activity was expected, because everyone using the system had specific government clearances, but there was no protection against accidents either, which, in my opinion, are more likely in such an environment.

Once logged into the system, OpenVMS supports three independent mechanisms that enforce system security. The three security mechanisms are access control list (ACL), user identification code (UIC), and system privileges. ACL is able to grant privileges on a user-by-user basis, or user groups can be defined to ease the manager's task. ACL, which is used to grant privileges to arbitrary groups, is governed by the rights identifier. ACL supersedes the others. If ACL does not specify an access privilege, then the UIC mechanism is examined. UIC grants privileges at the user level and/or at a predefined group level. The ACL and UIC mechanisms identify the system privilege of the user to access a specific resource in a specific way (e.g., no access, read-only, read/write).

Accounts and Passwords

Before discussing the account/password security mechanisms in detail, I will explain the major security components of an account. Before proceeding, you may want to refer to the basics of account creation discussed in Chapter 4.

The first defense of a secure system is to permit only authorized users to access it. The manager has several parameters to consider when defining his or her password policy. A few of these parameters were discussed in Chapter 4, but that list is incomplete. Here is a more extensive list. A reference to the controlling mechanism accompanies each item.

- Number of characters in the password: AUTHORIZE /PWDMINIMUM

- Number of passwords (0, 1, or 2) required at login time: AUTHORIZE / PASSWORD

- How often the user must change his or her password: AUTHORIZE / PWDLIFETIME

- The dictionary of unacceptable passwords: SYS$LIBRARY:VMS$PASSWORD_DICTIONARY.DATA

- A mechanism to enforce a password policy (e.g., to insist that the last character of the password must be a number): POLICY_PLAINTEXT.EXE written by manager

- Whether the system creates the user's password: AUTHORIZE/ FLAG=GENPWD

- Whether to maintain a password history (history prevents the user from alternating passwords): AUTHORIZE/FLAG=DISPWDHIS

- If a password history is maintained, how large should it be: DEFINE SYS$PASSWORD_HISTORY_LIMIT and DEFINE SYS$PASSWORD_HISTORY_LIFETIME

- Various aspects of the login process (i.e., how to handle invalid logins): SYSMAN PARAMETER LGI_xxx

- What hours the user may log in and by what means (e.g., dial-up, network, direct connection, batch): AUTHORIZE/PRIMEDAYS and AUTHORIZE/ ACCESS

- Whether the user operates from a controlled menu (captive account) or is free to use all DCL commands: AUTHORIZE/FLAGS=CAPTIVE

- Whether a user is permitted to receive mail: AUTHORIZE/FLAGS=DISMAIL

- Whether a user is permitted to log in: AUTHORIZE/FLAGS=DISUSER

- The manager's account, SYSTEM, may be restricted to log in to specific terminals: SET TERMINAL/PERMANENT/SYSPASSWORD

- System privileges granted to the account: AUTHORIZE/PRIVILEGE

- Membership in a logical group or groups for the purpose of security access: AUTHORIZE ADD/IDENTIFIER

Grouping Users to Enforce Security

Before explaining how security of resources works (in the next section), I must explain how users can be grouped. OpenVMS supports three grouping mechanisms:

- Individual users

- Groups based on user identification codes (UICs)

- Groups based on rights identifiers

For the sake of simplicity, the following examples are applied to files; however, as you read this section, remember that the same principles apply to the following resources:

- Common event flag clusters (simple semaphores)

- Global data sections

- Print and batch queues

- Devices (such as disk drives)

- Removable media (such as floppy disks and tapes), called volumes

- Logical tables

- Lock manager resources (complex semaphores)

Every user is assigned a UIC when entered into the SYSUAF. Refer to the UAF>SHOW DMILLER/FULL listing in Chapter 4. The second line of that display is:

```
Account:                            UIC:   [20,4] ([DMILLER])
```

The UIC on the right has two values: one numeric and the other alphanumeric. The numeric value is arbitrary and assigned by the manager. In this example, all users whose numeric UIC begins with 20 are in the same group. The alphanumeric is derived from the user name, of course, and has no inherent group designation in this case. The numeric group has meaning in the protection scheme. For instance, to examine the security level of one of my files, I would enter the following:

```
$ show security login.com

FACULTY:[DMILLER]LOGIN.COM;101 object of class FILE
    Owner: [DMILLER]
    Protection: (System: RWED, Owner: RWED, Group, World)
    Access Control List:
        (IDENTIFIER=[HICKEY],ACCESS=READ)
```

The first line displays the path name of the file. FACULTY is the name of the device. [DMILLER] in this context is the directory name. The file, LOGIN.COM, is in its 101st generation. The final phrase will be explained in the next section.

The second line specifies the alphanumeric UIC of the owner, [DMILLER], which happens to be the directory name and the account name.

The third line states the UIC protection levels; there are four in OpenVMS, not three as in UNIX. System refers to the system manager, and REWD is shorthand for Read-Execute-Write-Delete, meaning that all of those privileges are granted to System, and the Owner has the same privileges; however, the rest of the [20,*] group has no privileges, and neither do any of the other users (i.e., World). System and Owner may change the access privileges (i.e., Control privilege is automatically, and invisibly, granted). No flag is shown for UIC Control privilege.

The last two lines, the access control list, are described in the further discussion in this section.

Returning to UIC protection, I will demonstrate how to manipulate these fields. For instance, to change the UIC protection level to permit World read access to the file, DMILLER (or SYSTEM) would issue the command:

```
$ SET SECURITY/PROTECTION=(W:R) LOGIN.COM
```

To see the result, I have chosen an alternative command (DIR/SEC) to list the change. Also notice that I used abbreviations. This time the UIC protection is displayed in parentheses on the far right in a more cryptic form than the SHOW SECURITY command produces. The rightmost "R" is the World privilege just granted.

```
$ dir/sec login.com
```

```
Directory FACULTY:[DMILLER]

LOGIN.COM;101        [DMILLER]                              (RWED,RWED,,R)
          (IDENTIFIER=[HICKEY],ACCESS=READ)
```

ACLs are another way to control file access and, more generally, resource access. An ACL can be turned to either a specific user or to a rights list.

As it stands, one user, HICKEY, has read access to this file (i.e., before allowing world-read access). The following command adds another user, STUROSS, to the ACL list and displays the directory for the file again:

```
$ set sec/acl=(id=stuross,access=read) login.com

$ dir/sec login.com

Directory FACULTY:[DMILLER]

LOGIN.COM;101        [DMILLER]                              (RWED,RWED,,)
          (IDENTIFIER=[STUROSS],ACCESS=READ)
          (IDENTIFIER=[HICKEY],ACCESS=READ)
```

Rights Lists

An unprivileged user can control his or her files using ACL and UIC mechanisms, but only the manager can create arbitrary groups of users. This is done with a mechanism called the *rights identifier*. The use of a rights list makes management easier. Suppose I put STUROSS and HICKEY into a group named DM_RIGHT. Then the ACL list on this file becomes a single entry. The rights list is controlled by the manager with AUTHORIZE. Using groups based on the rights list is a three-step process:

- The manager creates the identifier.

- The manager associates the identifier with a number of users forming a group.

- The user (or the manager) creates an ACL for the identifier.

The following commands the manager would use to accomplish this task:

```
$ RUN AUTHORIZE
UAF> ADD/IDENTIFIER DM_RIGHT
UAF> sho /id dm_right
  Name                           Value           Attributes
  DM_RIGHT                       %X8001001B

UAF> GRANT/IDENT DM_RIGHT HICKEY
UAF> GRANT/ID DM_RIGHT STUROSS
UAF> sho /right/user=stuross
```

```
Identifier                            Value              Attributes
  DM_RIGHT                            %X8001001B
UAF> EXIT
```

Now DMILLER can issue the following commands

```
$ SET SEC/ACL=(id=DM_RIGHT,access=read) login.com

CSLab::DMILLER? sho sec login.com

FACULTY:[DMILLER]LOGIN.COM;101 object of class FILE
    Owner: [DMILLER]
    Protection: (System: RWED, Owner: RWED, Group, World)
    Access Control List:
        (IDENTIFIER=DM_RIGHT,ACCESS=READ)
```

Notice that there is some confusion between the identifier (i.e., the name of the rights-identifier) and the assignment of this right to a user. UAF>SHOW /ID lists the identifier, while UAF>SHO /RIGHT lists the user information. As you can see in the example, identifiers may have attributes, such as hiding the identifier name from the user.

Controlling Other Resources

As mentioned previously, security exists on eight classes of OpenVMS resources. Examples so far have been applied to files. Now we briefly look at some print queue examples. More specifically, the default privileges on a print queue permit a user to delete only his or her jobs; however, because security is managed on this resource, specific print queues may have certain characteristics altered. For instance, a user may be limited to a single printer or a group of printers. Thus, the granularity of the security ranges from a single user to a group of users to all users.

The default protection on a print queue is illustrated as follows. Each protection element shows the highest security level. For instance, System has Management (M) rights on the queue, and that includes all other rights. The Owner (who is SYSTEM in this case) has Job Delete (D) rights. The Group (i.e., SYSTEM again) has Read (R) rights, so all jobs in the queue may be displayed. The World has only Submit (S) rights. World cannot display jobs in the queue or manage the queue in any way. Notice also that an ACL is associated with the queue. This means that ACL protection discussed earlier can be applied to a specific user or group of users.

```
$ show sec /class=queue hotpink2

HOTPINK2 object of class QUEUE
    Owner: [SYSTEM]
    Protection: (System: M, Owner: D, Group: R, World: S)
    Access Control List: <empty>
```

In a trusted environment, the manager may want to elevate World privileges to permit any user to delete any job. So the manager could issue the following command:

```
$ set security /class=queue /protection=(W:RDS) hotpink2
```

which would result in the desired change.

```
$ show sec /class=queue hotpink2

HOTPINK2 object of class QUEUE
    Owner: [SYSTEM]
    Protection: (System: M, Owner: D, Group: R, World: DSR)
    Access Control List: <empty>
```

Alternately, the manager could also add a /PROTECTION clause to the INITIALIZE … HOTPINK2 command described in Chapter 5.

The reader may have noticed that the protection codes deviated from the expected RWED because of the capabilities of the resource. Likewise, if ACL access codes were used, they are expanded as well. For instance, one user could be given delete privilege to a particular queue, making this user the local printer operator.

Controlling Program Privileges

Beyond ACL and UIC privileges, 39 system privileges apply to system utilities and library routines. Two privileges—network mailbox creation permitted (NETMBX) and temporary mailbox creation permitted (TMPMBX)—are granted to all users. Two management policies are used to determine user privileges. The easiest way, which is wrong, is to grant all privileges to all users. This approach subverts many of the OpenVMS mechanisms and puts the system at risk. The right way to assign security privileges is on a user-by-user basis. This takes more effort on the manager's part but protects the system from both accidents and deliberate attacks.

To give the reader a flavor for how privileges interact with OpenVMS, here are some examples. Notice that not all privileges are concerned with file protection; more often, privileges are used to determine how closely a user may emulate management privileges. This is done by degrees and stages, not in a single step.

- ALTPRI (Alter Priority) permits the user to increase the priority level higher than specified in the SYSUAF. Priority is specified in commands SET PROCESS/PRIO=, RUN/DETACHED/PRIO=, and SUBMIT/PRIO=.

- EXQUOTA (Exceed Quota) permits the user to exceed disk quota when creating new files.

- BYPASS permits the user to skip all UIC privilege checks and grant access to any specified file.

- SETPRV (Set Privilege) permits the user to give him- or herself any privilege.

- VOLPRO (Volume Protection) permits the user to override volume protection and permits commands such as INITIALIZE to create a pristine volume structure.

Command descriptions in the HELP display and in the Compaq/HP manuals are clear regarding what privileges are required to perform certain functions and/or subfunctions. To emphasize these restrictions, error messages are likewise clear when those privileges are violated (e.g., if I attempt to initialize the system disk as an unprivileged user, the following dialog will result):

```
$ initialize dka100: mumble
%INIT-F-NOVOLPRO, operation requires VOLPRO privilege
```

Obviously, the VOLPRO privilege is required to initialize a disk, which is stated in the INITIALIZE command description.

Security Alarms and Audits

All of the security measures discussed protect the user from making stupid mistakes and protect the legitimate user community from malicious users and hackers. But protection is only the first step. The manager should be monitoring the various OpenVMS reports for security breaches as well. In the case of stupid mistakes, the manager may need to introduce better training directed at the specific user or toward a group of users. In the case of malicious security breach attempts, the manager may need to apprehend the offender or may want to tighten up security in certain areas.

The audit server, AUDIT_SERVER, is started automatically at boot time. It displays *alarms* on the operator console and records *audits* in SYS$MANAGER:SECURITY.AUDIT$JOURNAL. More than 20 events can cause an alarm and/or audit event. Alarms and audits can be enabled separately with the SET AUDIT command. To display which alarm and audit events are enabled, use SHOW AUDIT, as follows:

```
MANAGER> show audit
System security alarms currently enabled for:
  ACL
  Authorization
  Breakin:        dialup,local,remote,network,detached

System security audits currently enabled for:
  ACL
```

```
Authorization
Breakin:        dialup,local,remote,network,detached
Logfailure:     batch,dialup,local,remote,network,
                subprocess,detached
```

The audit information stored on disk is displayed by ANALYZE/AUDIT. The following displays show the same data in two formats. The first is a summary of all possible events, and the second provides more details about the six events. A third format, /FULL, displays even more data about a specific event.

```
MANAGER> analyze/audit/summary security.audit$journal

Total records read:        8          Records selected:           8
Record buffer size:      512
Successful logins:         0          Object creates:             0
Successful logouts:        0          Object accesses:            0
Login failures:            5          Object deaccesses:          0
Breakin attempts:          1          Object deletes:             0
System UAF changes:        0          Volume (dis)mounts:         0
Rights db changes:         0          System time changes:        0
Netproxy changes:          0          Server messages:            0
Audit changes:             2          Connections:                0
Installed db changes:      0          Process control audits:     0
Sysgen changes:            0          Privilege audits:           0
NCP command lines:         0

MANAGER> analyze/audit/brief security.audit$journal

Date / Time          Type        Subtype        Node    Username     ID
--------------------------------------------------------------------------------
 9-AUG-2002 00:00:56.17 AUDIT     AUDIT_LOG_FIRST BEAVER              00000000
 9-AUG-2002 07:39:01.36 LOGFAIL   REMOTE          CSWWW   <login>     208025C0
 9-AUG-2002 07:39:05.69 LOGFAIL   REMOTE          CSWWW   <login>     208025C0
 9-AUG-2002 07:39:09.99 LOGFAIL   REMOTE          CSWWW   <login>     208025C0
 9-AUG-2002 07:39:22.40 LOGFAIL   REMOTE          CSWWW   <login>     20802641
 9-AUG-2002 07:39:27.79 LOGFAIL   REMOTE          CSWWW   <login>     20802641
 9-AUG-2002 07:39:32.47 BREAKIN   REMOTE          CSWWW   AMGASSER1   20802641
10-AUG-2002 00:00:58.43 AUDIT     AUDIT_LOG_FINAL BEAVER              00000000
```

On the system I help manage, the audit file is restarted daily at midnight with the following command. Thus, the /BRIEF display shows those events as well.

```
$ set audit/server=new_log
```

Curiously, at the time I was preparing this example, user AMGASSER1 attempted to use his or her account. We disable student accounts during the summer, a fact the user apparently forgot. He or she tried so many times that a break-in was declared.

In addition to audit reports, the system manager may need to manage login violations. For instance, when a user login attempt reaches a given limit (this is a SYSMAN parameter), the user is prohibited from logging in even if done correctly for a certain time (another SYSMAN parameter). This usually occurs when novices are introduced to OpenVMS. The manager may monitor this action using SHOW INTRUSION.

```
$ show intrusion
```

Intrusion	Type	Count	Expiration	Source
TERMINAL	SUSPECT	3	2-AUG-2002 11:50:09.07	71.phoenix-13rh15rt- az.dial-access.att.net
NETWORK	INTRUDER	9	2-AUG-2002 11:58:37.87	LOON::DMILLER

Then the manager, using DELETE/INTRUSION, may remove the offending line, thus permitting the user to log in again without waiting for the timer to run down. For instance:

```
$ DELETE/INTRUSION LOON::DMILLER
```

Summary

- AUTHORIZE provides the manager with several ways to manage user access to the system.

- AUTHORIZE supports a database, called RIGHTSLIST.DAT, to group users in categories to ease management tasks.

- Users are also grouped by user identification code (UIC).

- Access control lists (ACLs) and UICs provide mechanisms to protect files, queues, devices, and other system resources from unauthorized access. SET PROTECTION is the primary command to assign protection levels to resources.

- Users can determine how the manager has set the various flags with SHOW PROCESS/ALL.

- SHOW INTRUSION is a DCL command to display the contents of the login intrusion (break-in) database.After ACL and UIC, system privileges act as an additional filter to determine certain resource protection, notably system-level management commands.

- DELETE/INTRUSION is a DCL command used to remove an entry from the intrusion database.

References

1. The primary security document is called *OpenVMS Guide to System Security.*

2. SHOW INTRUSION and SET SECURITY are documented fully in the *OpenVMS DCL Dictionary.*

3. The *OpenVMS System Manager's Manual* also discusses security from the manager's viewpoint.

4. All of the ANALYZE/AUDIT options are described in the *OpenVMS System Management Utilities Reference Manual*.

Chapter 9 — Network

OpenVMS has the capability to:

- Network computers with a variety of protocols.

- Configure, start, and stop protocols.

- Maintain display characteristics and usage, and tune protocols.

- Support various applications using the protocols.

- Manage network topology as defined by the protocol, such as routing and domain name servers.

- Manage security across the network.

OpenVMS supports several network protocols. Each one is managed separately. The rest of this chapter briefly describes each one. The reader is encouraged to carefully examine the Compaq/HP documentation before jumping into this subject. To give you a feel for the complexity of these products, one chapter is dedicated to each of these protocols in the *System Management Manual*. In addition, there are 11 more manuals for TCP/IP and 10 manuals for DECnet-Plus (also called DECnet Phase V). Thus, the following information is introductory.

TCP/IP

TCP/IP is familiar to all system managers. In OpenVMS its management has been automated through the use of a script. It can also be managed with a command-line interface of about 100 commands. Multinet and TCPW are also licensed TCP/IP stacks for OpenVMS.

The Compaq/HP-supported software is called TCP/IP version 5.3 at this writing. It is configured with a script called TCPIP$CONFIG and managed with the TCPIP command. When the system is booted, SYSTARTUP_VMS should be modified to include a line such as the following:

```
$ @SYS$STARTUP:TCPIP$STARTUP
```

The configuration script is shown in part, as follows. Once an option is selected, another menu is displayed. To illustrate the protocols supported by this version of TCP/IP, I selected the server option. This example and the ones following are not intended to be self-explanatory, and describing the concepts are beyond the scope of this book. These examples merely indicate the kind of interface the manager can expect.

```
$ @SYS$MANAGER:TCPIP$CONFIG

TCP/IP Network Configuration Procedure

This procedure helps you define the parameters required
to run Compaq TCP/IP Services for OpenVMS on this system.

Checking TCP/IP Services for OpenVMS configuration database files.

Compaq TCP/IP Services for OpenVMS Configuration Menu

Configuration options:
1 - Core environment
2 - Client components
3 - Server components
4 - Optional components
5 - Shutdown Compaq TCP/IP Services for OpenVMS
6 - Startup Compaq TCP/IP Services for OpenVMS
7 - Run tests
A - Configure options 1 - 4
[E] - Exit configuration procedure

Enter configuration option: 3
```

This option results in the following menu. Selecting one of these options causes another menu to display, but that is not shown.

```
Compaq TCP/IP Services for OpenVMS Server Components Configuration Menu
Configuration options:
     1 - BIND         Disabled Stopped   11 - NTP        Enabled Stopped
     2 - BOOTP        Disabled Stopped   12 - PC-NFS     Enabled Stopped
     3 - DHCP         Disabled Stopped   13 - POP        Enabled Stopped
     4 - FINGER       Enabled Stopped    14 - PORTMAPPER Enabled Stopped
     5 - FTP          Enabled Stopped    15 - RLOGIN     Enabled Stopped
     6 - LBROKER      Enabled Stopped    16 - RMT        Enabled Stopped
     7 - LPR/LPD      Enabled Stopped    17 - SNMP       Enabled Stopped
     8 - METRIC       Enabled Stopped    18 - TELNET     Enabled Stopped
     9 - NFS          Enabled Stopped    19 - TFTP       Enabled Stopped
    10 - LOCKD/STATD  Disabled Stopped   20 - XDM        Disabled Stopped
     A - Configure options 1 - 20
   [E] - Exit menu
Enter configuration option:
```

UNIX Connection (UCX) is an older version of TCP/IP and is frozen at version 4.2. Although it is no longer supported, some managers have not upgraded to the more recent version because they do not need the newer protocols (see the next example).

This version is set up with the script UCX$CONFIG and then managed with the UCX command. The SYSTARTUP_VMS startup script is @SYS$STARTUP:UCX$STARTUP. The disadvantage of this version is that it does not support some important protocols, such as serial line interface protocol (SLIP), which is used in conjunction with dial-up access to Internet service providers (ISPs).

To compare the two packages, the following example is exactly the same function as the previous TCP/IP example:

```
$ @ucx$config

                    TCP/IP Network Configuration Procedure

        This procedure helps you define the parameters required
        to run Digital TCP/IP Services for OpenVMS on this system.

        Checking TCP/IP Services for OpenVMS configuration database files.

        No new database files were created.

        Digital TCP/IP Services for OpenVMS Configuration Menu

        Configuration options:

                    1  -  Core environment
                    2  -  Client components
                    3  -  Server components
                    4  -  Optional components

                    5  -  Shutdown Digital TCP/IP Services for OpenVMS
                    6  -  Startup Digital TCP/IP Services for OpenVMS
                    7  -  Run tests

                    A  -  Configure options 1 - 3
                    [E]  -  Exit configuration procedure

    Enter configuration option: 3
```

Next, the screen is cleared and replaced by the following:

```
    Digital TCP/IP Services for OpenVMS SERVER Components Configuration Menu

        Configuration options:

                    1  -  BIND           Disabled
                    2  -  BOOTP          Disabled
                    3  -  TFTP           Disabled
                    4  -  FTP            Disabled
                    5  -  LPR/LPD        Disabled
                    6  -  NFS            Disabled
                    7  -  PC-NFS         Disabled
                    8  -  PORTMAPPER     Disabled
                    9  -  TELNET/RLOGIN  Enabled
                   10  -  SNMP           Disabled
                   11  -  NTP            Disabled
                   12  -  METRIC         Disabled
                   13  -  POP            Disabled
                   14  -  FINGER         Disabled
```

```
               A  -  Configure options 1 - 14
              [E]  -  Exit menu

     Enter configuration option:
```

Some servers (e.g., Finger, Network Time, Ping, FTP, SMTP) are included in TCP/IP for OpenVMS (depending on the version). Others, notably the HTTP server, can either be purchased from Compaq/HP or freeware (i.e., user-supported) can be downloaded. The community has also created servers and clients (e.g., Gopher, Finger, FTP, Ping, and SNTP) that predate those supplied by Compaq/HP. Kermit (a terminal emulator and a transfer protocol) will also run under OpenVMS.

DECnet

DECnet is a proprietary LAN and WAN protocol that has become a standard within the OpenVMS world. DECnet implements many of the TCP/IP protocols, and most of those predate TCP/IP. For instance, the asynchronous serial communications (SLIP in the TCP/IP world) called digital data communications message protocol (DDCMP) has been supported by DECnet for at least 20 years. DECnet security is far superior to TCP/IP even today; however, because DECnet is proprietary, it has never been very popular.

The newest package is called DECnet-Plus (sometimes called DECnet/OSI or DECnet V). It is set up with a script called NET$CONFIGURE and managed with the Network Command Language (NCL) command. When the system is booted, this version of DECnet starts automatically if it is installed.

A partial display of the set up script is as follows:

```
$ @sys$manager:net$configure basic

 Copyright (c) Digital Equipment Corporation 1993, 1996. All rights
 reserved.

     DECnet-Plus for OpenVMS BASIC network configuration procedure

 This procedure will help you create or modify the management scripts
 needed to operate DECnet on this machine. You may receive help about
 most questions by answering with a question mark '?'.

 You have chosen the BASIC configuration option.  This option enables
 you to quickly configure your system by answering a few questions and
 using most of the default answers.  If you would rather do some specific
 tailoring of your  system's network configuration, you should invoke
 NET$CONFIGURE.COM with the ADVANCED configuration option, ie:
             @SYS$MANAGER:NET$CONFIGURE ADVANCED

 Do you want to continue?                          [YES] :
 Enter the directory services to use on the system [LOCAL,DECDNS,DOMAIN] :
```

```
Enter the full name for directory service LOCAL    : LOCAL:.ELMER
Enter the full name for directory service DECDNS   : ACME:.WABBIT.ELMER
Enter the fully qualified host name for DNS/BIND   : ELMER.WABBIT.ACME.EDU
What type of node (Endnode or Router)?             [ENDNODE] :
Type of routing node (L1 or L2)?                        [L1] :
What is the synonym name for this node?            [ELMER] :
You have installed wide area device support, but it has not been
 configured.  You may configure it now if you want.

Do you want to configure Wide Area devices?             [YES] :
Are you satisfied with the answers you have given [Y] ?
```

Based on this dialog, NET$CONFIGURE builds an NCL script and then executes NCL using that data as input to initialize the DECnet database. Of course, the manager can enter the necessary operations interactively using NCL commands as well. The script is a labor-saving device.

The older version, DECnet IV, is still popular and supported. It is set up and managed with commands that are nearly the same as those of DECnet-Plus. The initialization script is called NETCONFIG (notice the $ is missing), and it is managed with Network Control Program (NCP). When the system is booted, it is initialized with a line in SYSTARTUP_VMS, @SYS$STARTUP:STARTNET.

The configuration script display is as follows:

```
$ @SYS$MANAGER:NETCONFIG.COM

DECnet for OpenVMS network configuration procedure

This procedure will help you define the parameters needed to get
DECnet running on this machine. You will be shown the changes before
they are actually executed, in case you wish to perform them manually.

What do you want your DECnet node name to be? :
What do you want your DECnet address to be? :
Do you want to operate as a router? [NO (nonrouting)]:
The network object database file is SYS$COMMON:[SYSEXE]NETOBJECT.DAT;4.
Do you want to purge the object database? [YES]:
Do you want a default DECnet account? [NO]:
Do you want a default account for the MAIL object? [YES]:
Do you want a default account for the FAL object? [NO]:
Do you want a default account for the PHONE object? [YES]:
Do you want a default account for the NML object? [YES]:
Do you want a default account for the MIRROR object? [YES]:
Do you want a default account for the VPM object? [YES]:
Do you want these commands to be executed? [YES]:
```

This dialog builds a script to be run by NCP to initialize the DECnet database.

To support the security of this product, two databases are supported. Associated with DECnet-Plus is a file called NET$PROXY.DAT, and with DECnet IV, it is called

NETPROXY.DAT. Both are managed with AUTHORIZE to permit users and processes DECnet access.

For instance, first assume that users have accounts on two nodes (say LOON and KEITH). The two nodes are connected with DECnet, but the nodes are not clustered together. Now, to permit any user on the LOON node to access his or her account on the KEITH with DECnet, the following AUTHORIZE command would be entered on KEITH:

```
$ MCR AUTHORIZE
UAF> ADD/PROXY LOON::* */DEFAULT
```

This permits any user logged in to LOON to perform DECnet operations such as the following:

```
$ COPY KEITH::ANYFILE.TXT  NEWFILE.TXT
$ TYPE KEITH::[.REPORTS]LISTFILE.DOC
```

The double-colon syntax signifies a node name, and directory syntax is also permitted. The manager would probably want to perform the same AUTHORIZE ADD/PROXY command on LOON as well to permit users to do symmetric operations.

DECnet syntax is recognized by any OpenVMS command that involves a file. DECnet is also recognized by several OpenVMS utilities (e.g., MOTIF, INITIALIZE/QUEUE, BACKUP, and EXCHANGE/NETWORK). MONITOR and SYSMAN are able to use DECnet to communicate between clustered nodes.

Local Area Network (LAN)

A LAN provides local services based on the 48-bit address of the network interface card (NIC) attached to the computer. In particular, maintenance operations protocol (MOP)—which is required for booting cluster satellites, print servers, and terminal servers—is offered by LAN. LAN also supports cluster monitoring and management functions provided with SYSMAN and MONITOR.

MOP is also included in DECnet, so LAN is unnecessary when DECnet is installed. On the other hand, DECnet is a separately licensed product, and LAN is included in the OpenVMS license, so if DECnet is not required, LAN can support MOP and cluster needs.

LAN is managed with LANCP and LANACP. The LAN Control Program (LANCP) is used to examine and modify the network device database, to manage performance, to control LANACP, and to initiate MOP messages. For this purpose, LANCP supports about 20 commands. For instance, to show information about a device, the following command will produce a display similar to the following:

```
LANCP> SHOW DEVICE/COUNTERS EXA0:
Device Counters EXA0:
    Value    Counter
    -----    -------
   259225    Seconds since last zeroed
  5890496    Data blocks received
  4801439    Multicast blocks received
   131074    Receive failure
764348985    Bytes received
543019961    Multicast bytes received
        3    Data overrun
  1533610    Data blocks sent
   115568    Multicast packets transmitted
   122578    Blocks sent, multiple collisions
    86000    Blocks sent, single collision
   189039    Blocks sent, initially deferred
198120720    Bytes sent
 13232578    Multicast bytes transmitted
  7274529    Send failure
        0    Collision detect check failure
        0    Unrecognized frame destination
        0    System buffer unavailable
        0    User buffer unavailable
```

The LAN Auxiliary Control Program (LANACP) is the server (or symbiont or daemon) that receives messages from other nodes.

Local Area Transport (LAT)

LAT, another DEC proprietary protocol, is optimized for terminal servers for dumb terminals, printers, and modems. As with LAN, it is based on the 48-bit NIC address. TCP/IP is usually available on terminal servers as well, but LAT is more efficient because it can multiplex several terminal messages into a single network message.

LAT was developed specifically for dumb terminal communication (via terminal servers). LAT was designed to be very fast; hence, it will not tolerate WAN delays of any sort. Furthermore, the protocol has no provision to be routed or bridged. Of course, dumb terminals are not a popular item these days, so LAT's popularity has likewise waned.

LAT is managed with the LAT Control Program (LATCP); however, LAT creates and maintains its own network database through "keep alive" messages that it sends out (and receives) periodically; thus, it does not need a domain name server. Examples in Chapter 5 regarding print queues show examples of LATCP commands. The manager edits LAT$SYSTARTUP.COM, and the script SYS$STARTUP:LAT$STARTUP will start up automatically. Instructions for doing this are embedded in the files.

An example of an LATCP display is as follows. This command lists all nodes on the network running LAT.

```
$ MCR LATCP

LATCP> show node /all

 LAT Control Program
Node Name          Status        Identification
----------------   -----------   -------------------------------
BEAVER             On            .HS 104 -- OpenVMS V7.1
CSWWW              Reachable     .HS 104 -- OpenVMS V7.1
EAGLE              Reachable     OpenVMS/Alpha, Version V7.1
HERON              Reachable     OpenVMS/Alpha, Version V7.1
LOON               Reachable     .HS 104 -- OpenVMS V7.1
```

Summary

- TCP/IP services are supported by a product called Compaq TCP/IP Services for OpenVMS.

- Third-party TCP/IP products are also available.

- Two DECnet versions are supported: DECnet-Plus and DECnet Phase IV (or simply DECnet).

- MOP, a boot protocol, is supported by DECnet and LAN.

- LAT is a fast server protocol.

Related Publications

1. The top-level document is *Compaq TCP/IP Services for OpenVMS Concepts and Planning*. It points to the other ten (or more) that are available.

2. For DECnet, the top-level document is *DECnet-Plus for OpenVMS Introduction and User's Guide*. It references nine additional documents.

3. LANCP and LATCP are documented in *OpenVMS System Management Utilities Reference Manual: A–L*.

4. Networking in more general terms is discussed in Chapters 23 through 26 of the *OpenVMS System Manager's Manual, Volume 2: Tuning, Monitoring, and Complex Systems*.

Chapter 10 — Clusters

OpenVMS has the capability to:

- Create and manage a cluster of CPUs interconnected with various LAN options.

- Share resources within the cluster, such as printers and files.

- Share system management structures, such as user account file (SYSUAF), mail profile, and so on.

- Support widely dispersed clusters.

- Support multipathed disk farms.

- Support system management of all CPUs from a single node.

- Support diskless nodes.

The OpenVMS Cluster is an OpenVMS feature that permits multiple (up to about 100) computers to be interconnected and to invisibly share resources such as software packages, printers, files, and devices. A cluster also provides a fail-safe operation for the computing facility, because a cluster can be configured to run without a full complement of computers. A cluster might be distributed over several miles and, if the connection between them is severed, the reduced cluster can continue operation (with reduced capacity) in a matter of seconds, as if nothing had happened. Furthermore, once the connection is restored, the cluster melds itself back into a single unit.

OpenVMS out of the box supports clusters. This is not an add-on product and is designed into OpenVMS, although it requires a separate license. Clusters (in the OpenVMS sense) are made up of several computers cooperatively sharing resources. A single copy of the operating system usually resides on one cluster member. All of the members of the cluster are managed and operate under the same security domain (i.e., with a single user authorization database). Thus, the system manager can access any CPU from any other one for management purposes using the SYSMAN command. A user logs in to all CPUs the same way and has the same privileges throughout the cluster. When an application is started, it may execute on a single CPU or, if it is coded correctly, on multiple CPUs. In the latter case the processes must cooperate to access shared resources. A given disk drive can be either made local to one CPU or can be globally read/write accessed by any member of the cluster. In the latter case a clusterwide locking mechanism controls and synchronizes access requests across the cluster.

A cluster is similar to a symmetric multiprocessor (SMP) computer in that most of the cluster's resources can be shared. A cluster is unlike an SMP computer in that each cluster member has its own memory and, optionally, its own disk drive(s). Memory of the individual CPUs cannot be shared, but disks may be. Furthermore, the cluster should be configured so that any member computer can be stopped (e.g., for repairs) and then rebooted into the cluster again without any interruption to the other computers in the cluster. Therefore, critical processes on the stopped computer (e.g., the queue manager) fail-over automatically to a running node.

Creating a Simple Cluster

To begin, let us build a simple cluster. Suppose that several Alphas are connected to an Ethernet network and each computer has a hard drive. Now suppose that OpenVMS is installed on just one of those computers and it is booted (leave the others alone for now). After loading licenses and so forth, this computer can be made into a one-node cluster. Creating a cluster with one member is done with a script called CLUSTER_CONFIG, which displays the following information and menu. This script would be used to create the Boot Server and a File Server for the cluster.

```
MANAGER> @cluster_config

                    Cluster Configuration Procedure
                      Executing on a Alpha System

    This system is running DECnet Phase IV.

    DECnet will be used for MOP downline loading.

        Use CLUSTER_CONFIG.COM to set up or change an OpenVMS Cluster
        Configuration.
        To ensure that this procedure is executing with the required
        privileges, invoke it from the system manager's account.

        Enter a "?" for help at any prompt.  If you are familiar with
        the execution of this procedure, you may want to mute extra notes
        and explanations by invoking it with "@CLUSTER_CONFIG BRIEF".


        EAGLE is an Alpha system
        so the following functions can be performed:

    MAIN MENU

        1. ADD an Alpha node to the cluster.
        2. REMOVE a node from the cluster.
        3. CHANGE a cluster member's characteristics.
        4. CREATE a duplicate system disk for EAGLE.
        5. EXIT from this procedure.
```

There are several more steps in the procedure that are not included in the example. The system manager specifies the following:

- The node's name and address

- Whether the node is to be a boot server (if not, the name of the boot server)

- Whether the node is to be a file server (if not, the name of the file server)

- The name of the node's root of the system directory tree

- The voting information used for the cluster integrity algorithm

After the single-node cluster is formed, the manager would probably want to install layered products, such as TCP/IP, C++, and so on, and license them. Again, these products only have to be installed and licensed once for all of the nodes, but the licenses must have enough units for all of the nodes. See Chapter 3 for the license discussion. The manager must also create accounts for the users of the cluster. All services installed on EAGLE are available on all of the nodes without any special considerations.

Finally, to add the other nodes, use CLUSTER_CONFIG again for each one. These nodes are called *satellites*. Nodes may be either VAX or Alpha computers, with no restrictions on CPU speed, memory size, or devices connected to the node (e.g., both a VAX without a display or keyboard and only 12 megabytes of memory and an Alpha with display, keyboard, and mouse and several hundred megabytes of memory may be cluster members). Depending on the interconnect communications hardware configuration, up to 95 satellites can be added to the cluster. The interconnect between computers determines the limit of the number of nodes, as detailed in the next section. As CLUSTER_CONFIG is run, the manager will be instructed to boot the satellite, and it will automatically configure itself for the physical characteristics of the particular machine. In other words, the satellites do not have to be identical to EAGLE in any way. Each one can have a different CPU model, a different amount of memory, and a different number of disks. With special care a satellite can be a VAX instead of an Alpha. This configuration is not discussed further.

After all of the nodes have been configured, the cluster will have the following characteristics:

- When a satellite boots, EAGLE will serve the boot programs using Maintenance Operations Protocol (MOP) and then serve all OpenVMS files as required using Mass Storage Control Protocol (MSCP).[1]

---

1. MSCP is a disk-independent read/write communications protocol designed to make all disk I/O requests uniform. The disk server translates the MSCP message into disk-specific operations.

- When a user logs into a satellite (or the server), SYSUAF, the login scripts, and the other files required to affect the login process will be served to the satellite.

- The user's process will be created on that satellite and will reside there until the session is complete.

- Any files accessed by that user will be served from EAGLE.

- Commands entered by the user will cause images to be loaded from EAGLE into the satellite's memory for execution.

- Assuming the queue manager is running on EAGLE, print and batch requests will be transferred to EAGLE for processing.

- The cluster-locking mechanism will control access to a file by more than one user, even write accesses.

- As more users log in to the cluster, the load will be balanced across the satellites. OpenVMS assigns new users to the least utilized node.

Failure of a satellite node or the network segment connecting a node to the cluster will not affect the cluster's performance, only the single node. Depending on how the cluster is set up, a user's session on the failed node can be forced to roll over to another node; however, failure of EAGLE will cause the entire cluster to collapse, because it is the file server for all nodes.

Complex Clusters

If higher cluster reliability is a concern—and this is where cluster technology can be extremely beneficial—several options are available to reduce system downtime to mere seconds:

- To reduce the risk of disk failures, they can be shadowed.

- To reduce the risk of disk and tape controller failures, use double-ported disk controllers.

- To reduce the risk of server CPU-to-disk path and CPU-to-tape path failures, replicate the path.

- To reduce the risk of server CPU failures, include additional CPUs using the replicated device paths.

- To reduce the risk of CPU-to-CPU communication failure, replicate the paths.

- To reduce the risk of data center failures, replicate the data center.

A large variety of supported hardware options are available to implement any portion or all of the previous list. These options run across the cost-performance spectrum and are described briefly as follows. No matter what particular solution is selected, recovery from any of these failures takes only seconds to perform. That is, if any of the failures listed occur, the cluster will reconfigure itself in at most seconds and often faster.

The following hardware implementations can be used to connect cluster nodes together:

- *Asynchronous Transfer Mode (ATM).* 155 megabits per second with 2-kilometer separation or 622 megabits per second and 300-meter separation; 96 node maximum

- *Ethernet.* 10 megabits per second with 100-meter separation, 100 megabits per second with 100-meter separation, or 1,000 megabits per second and 550-meter separation; 96 node maximum

- *Fiber Distributed Data Interface (FDDI).* 100 megabits per second with 40-kilometer separation; 96 node maximum

- *Computer Interconnect (CI).* 140 megabits per second (70 MB/s on each path) and 45-meter separation; 32 node maximum. This interconnect requires a star coupler.

- *DIGITAL Storage Systems Interconnect (DSSI).* 32 megabits per second and 8-meter separation; four node maximum. Four integrated storage elements (ISEs)—that is, disk controllers—can also be attached.

- *Memory Channel (MC).* 800 megabits per second and 2-meter separation; four node maximum

- *Small Computer System Interface (SCSI).* 160 megabits per second and 25-meter separation; 16 node maximum

- *Fibre Channel (FC).* 1,000 megabits per second and 100-kilometer separation; 96 node maximum

In addition to interconnecting CPUs, some of these hardware solutions will also connect to disk and tape controllers. Called hierarchical storage controllers (HSCs), these are intelligent controllers designed to support RAID operations (level 0 striping, 1 shadowing, 5 striping with parity), as well as support cluster operations. OpenVMS will support these RAID operations in the event that HSCs are not used. Thus, HSCs provide multiple-path disks and shadowed and/or striped disks.

Cluster Quorum

If a cluster is fragmented into two (or more) parts, the data (disk and tape) integrity must be protected. For instance, a database application may be running on separate CPUs at two data centers several miles apart for safety reasons. The common database is stored in a volume shadow set configuration, RAID 1, with some disks at each site. In normal operation, both sites interrogate and update the database, and the changes to the database are duplicated (or mirrored) in both places. If the link between the sites is disrupted, however, one data center must shut itself down so that the composite database does not diverge.

Deciding which data center (or which CPU) is to control the database is done with a quorum mechanism. This is how it works: Each file server node in the clusters has a vote, but satellites do not. The system manager determines the minimum number of votes (the quorum) possible for continued cluster operation. A cluster component called the Quorum Watcher on each node monitors the cluster quorum and signals a shutdown when the cluster drops below the minimum number of votes. It is essential that the manager understand this algorithm. It is detailed in all of the cluster manuals.

Cluster Management

To control and monitor the cluster, the manager has several tools, three of which are illustrated as follows. Return to the simple cluster example with EAGLE as the boot server and file server and BEAVER, LOON, and WWW as satellites. To confirm the health of his or her system, the manager can use the following command (this is the primary command used to examine the status of a cluster):

```
$ SHOW CLUSTER

View of Cluster from system ID 64518  node: LOON 4-AUG-2002 18:54:49
+---------------------------+
*       SYSTEMS        * MEMBERS *
+-------------------+---------*
*  NODE  * SOFTWARE *  STATUS *
+--------+----------+---------*
* LOON   * VMS V7.3 * MEMBER  *
* BEAVER * VMS V7.3 * MEMBER  *
* EAGLE  * VMS V7.3 * MEMBER  *
* WWW    * VMS V7.3 * MEMBER  *
+---------------------------+
```

Notice that this display was created when logged into LOON, not EAGLE. SHOW CLUSTER is a rich command with several subcommands. Only three fields—NODE, SOFTWARE, and STATUS—are shown. There are nearly 100 fields available for display. SHOW CLUSTER can be run continuously or provide only a cluster snapshot. Both status and performance data can be displayed.

Another way to examine the performance of the cluster members is with the MONITOR CLUSTER command. The following display shows four performance components of the top six nodes in the cluster:

- CPU utilization expressed in busy percentage

- Memory utilization expressed in percentage

- Disk I/O rate in operations per second

- Resource lock rate in operations per second

```
$ MONITOR CLUSTER

Statistic: CURRENT            OpenVMS Monitor Utility      4-AUG-2002 18:55:37
                                  CLUSTER STATISTICS
                        CPU                 |            MEMORY

CPU Busy          0    25   50   75  100|%Memory In Use  0    25   50   75  100
                  +----+----+----+----+|                +----+----+----+----+
LOON            1 |                      |WWW         47 |********
WWW             1 |                      |LOON        44 |********
EAGLE           1 |                      |BEAVER      19 |***
BEAVER            |                      |EAGLE       14 |**
                  |                      |
                  |                      |
                  |                      |
-------------------------------------------+-------------------------------------
                        DISK                |            LOCK

I/O Operation Rate 0    25   50   75  100|Tot ENQ/DEQ Rate 0   125  250  375  500
                   +----+----+----+----+|                 +----+----+----+----+
LOON$DKA0:            |                   |LOON             |
BEAVER$DKA0:    R    |                   |BEAVER           |
EAGLE$DKA0:     R    |                   |EAGLE            |
EAGLE$DKB0:     R    |                   |WWW              |
EAGLE$DKB100:   R    |                   |                 |
WWW$DKA0:       R    |                   |                 |
```

This real-time display is updated every six seconds to show the dynamics of the cluster. MONITOR can display more than 20 other resources. MONITOR can also record and/or average these statistics.

The following SHOW DEVICE display shows the devices (in this case, only disks) served from node BEAVER. Mass Storage Control Protocol (MSCP) is used to remotely access disk files and Tape Mass Storage Control Protocol (TMSCP) is used to remotely access tape files.

```
MANAGER> show device/served/host
        MSCP-Served Devices on BEAVER 24-AUG-2002 12:04:37.22

                                           Queue Requests
Device:          Status     Total Size    Current    Max     Hosts
    DKA0         Online        4110480           0      2         3
    DKA100       Avail         4110480           0      0         0

                                           Queue Requests
Host:                 Time of Connection   Current    Max    Devices
    LOON         25-JUN-2002 10:07:18.41         0      5         1
    WWW          25-JUN-2002 10:20:26.05         0      4         1
    EAGLE        13-AUG-2002 13:31:40.32         0      2         1

        TMSCP-Served Devices on BEAVER 24-AUG-2002 12:04:37.28

                                           Queue Requests
Device:          Status     Position      Current    Max     Hosts
TMSCP-Server code not loaded
```

Summary

- CLUSTER_CONFIG is the primary script used to create and manage clusters.

- SHOW CLUSTER and MONITOR CLUSTER are tools used by the manager to examine status and performance of the cluster.

- Cluster design is an important effort involving many performance and cost tradeoffs.

- Once created, the cluster can be expanded easily. This is an inexpensive way to expand data center capability because existing components do not have to be scrapped.

Related Publications

1. A thorough discussion of the various vendors' cluster software is found in *In Search of Clusters* by Gregory Pfister. This book is considered to be the "cluster Bible" by many users, because it gives a fair treatment of all important products as of the publication date (circa 1999).

2. A brief PowerPoint presentation of cluster comparisons (circa 2000) can be downloaded from eisner.decus.org/lugs/esilug/presentations/.

3. Before setting up your first cluster, read *Guidelines for OpenVMS Cluster Configurations. OpenVMS Cluster Systems* contains several detailed examples of setting up and maintaining clusters in Chapter 8.

4. *Volume Shadowing for OpenVMS* is a necessary companion to complete the clustering topic.

5. Chapter 22 of the *OpenVMS System Manager's Manual, Volume 2: Tuning, Monitoring, and Complex Systems* is a good introduction to clusters and some management issues.

6. MONITOR and SHOW CLUSTER are fully described in the *OpenVMS System Management Utilities Reference Manual: M–Z.*

7. The OpenVMS technical reference was written by Roy Davis in 1993, called *VAX Cluster Principles*. Although dated, the basic algorithms and data structures are still valid, even though new hardware capabilities have been added.

Bibliography

Digital/Compaq/HP Manuals

The Compaq/HP document titles do not follow any particular standard, so the content is sometimes difficult to imagine by reading the title only. Furthermore, I find the packing of several manuals under a single title to be occasionally confusing. So I have added some helpful comments to each title to help you recognize its worth. When all else fails, start your search in the *Master Index*. It is very thorough and accurate. Most of these can be found online at www.openvms.compaq.com:8000.

Compaq Availability Manager User's Guide

> This product is a GUI for account, disk, and queue management. It can be run from either an OpenVMS terminal or a Windows terminal.

Compaq DECprint Supervisor (DCPS) for OpenVMS

> This is not currently available online. This product is licensed with the OpenVMS license.

Compaq OpenVMS Operating System for Alpha and VAX, Version 7.3

> This is the software product description (SPD) for OpenVMS 7.3.

Compaq TCP/IP Services for OpenVMS Concepts and Planning

> This is the top-level TCP/IP document. It points to the other ten (or more) that are available.

Compaq TCP/IP Services for OpenVMS Management

> This is an invaluable tutorial for OpenVMS TCP/IP. In particular, TCP/IP network printers are discussed in Part 6.

Compaq TCP/IP Services for OpenVMS Tuning and Troubleshooting

> *TCP/IP Services* includes extensive performance collection capabilities. This manual shows how to monitor and tune TCP/IP effectively and in detail.

DECnet for OpenVMS Networking Manual

This is the "Bible" for DECnet IV.

DECnet-Plus for OpenVMS Introduction and User's Guide

This references nine additional DECnet-Plus documents.

DECnet-Plus for OpenVMS Network Management

This is the DECnet V management authority. It also discusses migration from DECnet IV to DECnet V.

Guide to OpenVMS File Applications

Describes OpenVMS Record Management System (RMS) file types and their applications.

OpenVMS Alpha System Analysis Tools Manual

Details the Alpha implementation of the system dump analyzer (SDA).

OpenVMS Command Definition, Librarian, and Message Utilities Manual

This manual is actually a collection of three unrelated utilities:

1. *Command Definition* describes the mechanism that OpenVMS uses to parse command parameters for processing by an application.

2. The *Librarian* is a utility used throughout OpenVMS for various types of libraries. This manual details use of the LIBRARY command.

3. All OpenVMS messages are managed via a database. Compaq/HP recommends that user-written applications also use that database for consistency, and this manual describes how to do it.

OpenVMS DCL Dictionary

This is an unlikely title for the manual that describes many of the Digital Command Language (DCL) commands and their options. It includes numerous examples as well. It is a two-volume set (i.e., A–M and N–Z).

OpenVMS Guide to System Security

This is a philosophy book as well as a detailed how-to book. Use this book when formulating site security, because DEC engineers have solutions for situations that have never crossed your mind.

OpenVMS License Management Utility Manual

This manual describes software licensing philosophy generally. It also includes a description of the LICENSE command.

OpenVMS Management Station Overview and Release Notes

This management software runs on a PC. This document is only a brief description. Full documentation is available, once it is installed on the PC, under the HELP feature.

OpenVMS Master Index

This is an invaluable index, because it cross-references a given topic to the several documents that discuss it. Furthermore, its subheadings are detailed so that often only one probe will lead you to the desired material.

The OpenVMS online HELP facility is easy to use and complete. It includes many examples and complements the *OpenVMS DCL Dictionary* primarily.

OpenVMS Performance Management

This book begins with a philosophical discussion of operating system performance. A manager cannot deal with statements such as, "My program takes too long to execute" very well. The manager is encouraged to ask the right questions before attempting to change any of the OpenVMS parameters. Then it describes the OpenVMS tuning algorithms extensively. In the process of describing the algorithms, it describes how to use the performance programs available with OpenVMS.

OpenVMS Software Overview

Although a bit dated now, this introductory document defines and illustrates many of the OpenVMS capabilities and features.

OpenVMS System Management Utilities Reference Manual

This is another collection of independent manuals required to manage the system, divided into two volumes (i.e., A–L and M–Z). This manual picks up where the *DCL Dictionary* leaves off. That is, normal users do not have any business poking around in this collection because they are not privileged enough to use them. It includes the various system management utilities needed every day (e.g., ACCOUNTING, ANALYZE/AUDIT, AUTHORIZE, BACKUP,

DECevent, LANCP, LATCP, and SYSMAN) and describes them completely with many examples.

OpenVMS System Manager's Manual: Volume 1: Essentials

This is the manager's primary reference.

OpenVMS System Manager's Manual: Volume 2: Tuning, Monitoring, and Complex Systems

This is the manager's other primary reference, actually a continuation of Volume 1, a mere packing ploy. If the two were bound together (think hard copy), it would be too awkward to manage.

OpenVMS VAX System Dump Analyzer Utility Manual

Details the VAX implementation of system dump analyzer (SDA).

Volume Shadowing for OpenVMS

This manual discusses all aspects of shadowing, including how to back up a shadow set, with many examples.

WWW Resources

I hesitate to add this section because, since the HP acquisition, urls are bound to change. These addresses are currently valid, and I would like to hope that Compaq/HP will maintain them in the future.

Software product description (SPD) home page is at www.compaq.com/info/spd.

OpenVMS and layered product patches are found at ftp://ftp1.service.digital.com/public/vms. This site includes both VAX and AXP (Alpha) patches for many versions of OpenVMS. Each patch includes a README and installation instructions.

License units required for all VAXes and Alphas can be found online at www.compaq.com/products/software/info/ in the Reference Material tab. This location contains lots of other information regarding licenses.

I've found the best starting point to reach the user community is www.levitte.org/~ava/. This site seems to point to everything else available, including DEC/Compaq/HP sites.

Hunter Goatley maintains one of the best OpenVMS software collections at www.process.com/openvms/index.html.

The official FAQ site is www.openvms.compaq.com/wizard/openvms_faq.html. This information is actively updated regularly; however, this is not the only FAQ site available. See www.levitte.org/~ava/vms_faq.htmlx for others.

Hewlett-Packard maintains OpenVMS training for system managers online at www.openvms.compaq.com/training.html.

The site www.multimania.com/pmoreau/decw/decw.html is the source of many freeware Motif packages that may interest the system manager.

The prime OpenVMS hackers' homepage is deathrow.vistech.net/. It would be smart to read over that material and ensure that you are protected against any of the possible problems described.

Books

Digital Press, CBM Books (which is now part of Digital Press), and others published many VMS (and OpenVMS) titles when DEC hardware and software were in their prime, but many (but not all) of the titles listed are out of print today. Clearly, Digital Press is still active in the OpenVMS market. Be sure to read the back cover for a list of the latest Digital Press books.

Anagnostopoulos, Paul C., and Steve Hoffman. *Writing Real Programs in DCL*, second edition. Digital Press, 1999, ISBN 1555581919.

> The is the command language "Bible." It is required reading for system managers.

Baldwin, Lawence. *OpenVMS System Management Guide*. Digital Press, 1996, ISBN 1555581439.

> This is a concise yet complete description of the *System Manager's Manual*. Most commonly performed operations are covered. A second edition is in the publication cycle.

Bell, C. Gordon, J. Craig Mudge, and John E. McNamara. *Computer Engineering: A DEC View of Hardware Systems Design*. Digital Press, 1978, IBSN 0932376002.

> Contains the nitty-gritty of the hardware design constraints DEC hardware engineers had to manage. Gordon Bell was DEC's chief hardware architect. Although technologically dated, Bell's general observations probably still hold in computer design today.

Coburn, James W. *OpenVMS Performance Management*, second edition. CBM Books, 1994, ISBN 187895640X.

This book addresses specific algorithms used to test and adjust OpenVMS. Because it is dated, this text should be used in conjunction with *OpenVMS Performance Management*.

Davis, Roy G. *VAXCluster Principles*. Digital Press, 1993, ISBN 1555581129.

Clustered VAXes were introduced in 1983, so the algorithms and data structures presented in this book still hold true; however, newer hardware architecture will not be included.

Goldenberg, Ruth E., Denise E. Dumas, and Saro Saravana. *OpenVMS Alpha Internals: Scheduling and Process Control*. Digital Press, 1997, ISBN 1555581560.

A detailed description of OpenVMS data structures is found in "the book of Ruth." The earlier titles were either *VAX/VMS Internals and Data Structures* or *OpenVMS Internals and Data Structures*, depending on the edition. This book is republished often to keep up with newer versions of OpenVMS. The latest complete VAX/VMS edition is for Version 5.5-2. The latest complete Alpha/VMS edition is for Version 1.5. This newest Alpha edition has been partially updated and will continue to be updated.

Holmay, Patrick. *The OpenVMS User's Guide*, second edition. Digital Press, 1998, ISBN 1555582036.

If you've never used OpenVMS before, this is the best introduction available. OpenVMS's basic commands, editors, the file structure, and an introduction to Command Procedures (i.e., script writing) are included.

Miller, David Donald. *OpenVMS Operating System Concepts*, second edition. Digital Press, 1997, ISBN 1555581579.

Describes several basic operating system concepts (e.g., paging, lock management, process communication, and the I/O kernel) and illustrates them using OpenVMS. If you do not know how operating systems work, read this book before tackling Goldenberg.

Ogilvie, Lesley Rice, David W. Bynon, and Terry C. Shannon. *Introduction to OpenVMS*, fourth edition. CBM Books, 1996, ISBN 1878956612.

This is another introductory OpenVMS book directed at the novice. The fifth edition (I have not see it) is published by Digital Press. This book gives a cursory treatment of OpenVMS (more so than Holmay's *User's Guide*) but covers a broader range of topics, including Motif and some management issues.

Pearson, Jamie (ed.). *Digital At Work: Snapshots from the First Thirty-Five Years.* Digital Press, 1992, ISBN 1555580920.

This is a composite of recollections by folks who participated in DEC's successes. The book includes some great pictures. It was published in 1992, so no Alpha stories are included.

Rifkin, Glenn, and George Harrar. *The Ultimate Entrepreneur: The Story of Ken Olsen and Digital Equipment Corporation.* Contemporary Books, 1988, ISBN 0809245590.

Ken Olsen's biography—and Digital's too, of course—is recorded here. It was published in 1988, during DEC's heyday, so it's not the whole story. The Alpha development is missing completely.

If you found this book useful, you'll want to explore the resources provided in other Digital Press books as well. In the appendices that follow, we offer you excerpts from these OpenVMS titles:

- Michael D. Duffy, *Getting Started with OpenVMS: A Guide for New Users*, 1-55558-279-6, Digital Press, 2002

- Alan Winston, *OpenVMS with Apache, OSU, and WASD: The Nonstop Webserver*, 1-55558-264-8, Digital Press, 2002

- John Robert Wisniewski, *Linux and OpenVMS Interoperability: Tricks for Old Dogs, New Dogs, and Hot Dogs with Open Systems*, 1-55558-267-2, Digital Press, 2003

- Ruth E. Goldenberg, *OpenVMS Alpha Internals and Data Structures: Memory Management*, 1-55558-159-5, Digital Press, 2002

- Paul C. Anagnostopoulos and Steve Hoffman, *Writing Real Programs in DCL, 2nd Edition*, 1-55558-191-9, Digital Press, 1999

Digital Press is proud to publish the definitive list of titles on all critical aspects of OpenVMS.

These books and other related publications are available through online and brick-and-mortar booksellers, or at www.digitalpressbooks.com.

Appendix A — The User Environment

By Michael D. Duffy

This chapter will discuss the OpenVMS user environment; how to work with files, directories, printers, and batch queues; and how to run programs and perform other common tasks.

As with earlier sections in this book, the DCL CLI interface will be used. Most common functions may also be carried out using a GUI interface.

Files

Most OpenVMS operations act on files, the primary unit of data storage. With few exceptions, all data processed by the system reside, at one time or another, in files. An understanding of files is essential to using most operating systems. Our description of the OpenVMS environment will begin with files.

Definition of a File

The *file* is the central unit of data storage. Programs, letters, memos, pictures, audio clips, and just about any other type of data are stored in files. A single file usually represents a single entity: one file per picture, one file per audio clip, etc. However, some file formats support the storage of multiple entities within a file. Examples of the latter are backup savesets, libraries, and zip files.

Compare this to a popular method of presenting data—the Web page. A given Web page may contain pictures, text, sounds, and other elements. This may give the illusion that all of these types of data are stored together as a single unit. In reality, each of these elements is stored in a separate file; they are presented together by the browser program at the time of viewing.

A file is a single logical unit on a computer storage device (e.g., a disk or tape) and is made up of *records*. A given file may consist of records of varying length (e.g., lines in a memo or letter) or each record may have a fixed length. A record may be divided into smaller units called *fields*. An employee name, a telephone number, or an identification number may be a field within a record, and all related records (say, one for each employee of a company) comprise a file.

OpenVMS supports many different file and record formats. Most other systems provide relatively few formats, so new users of OpenVMS may not be familiar with all of them. In addition, users familiar with other operating systems may be accustomed to slightly different definitions of some key terms. These terms are presented here as they are used with OpenVMS.

Within the file organizations listed below, there are many possible variations of the control information used to describe each record. These variations are not addressed in this book. They are handled automatically by OpenVMS Record Management Services (RMS) and the file system and are of little concern to the new user.

The overwhelming majority of files you will encounter will be sequential files. This is true for experienced users as well as novices. When you do come across files of other organizations, they will be for a specific purpose and will most often be managed by a particular piece of software.

As a new user, you will rarely need to know the details of a file's organization or of the record format within it. They are presented here mainly for informational purposes.

Sequential

Most files on a given OpenVMS system are sequential. As their name implies, they are suitable for sequential processing. That is, every record is expected to be processed in order from the beginning to the end of the file. Please note that they are expected, but not required, to be processed in this way.

There are two main variations of record formats used with a sequential file: variable-length and fixed-length. With variable-length records, the records within the file may differ in size from one another. This means that records in the file must usually be processed from the beginning of the file, one at a time, going toward the end of the file. Records may be added to the end of the file, but usually not inserted at an earlier point. Inserting records is usually accomplished by rewriting the entire file, but theoretically this can be done by rewriting all records from the point of insertion onward.

With fixed-length records, all of the records in the file are the same length. Even though the file is sequential, it is possible to retrieve a given record without reading the file from the beginning, because one may mathematically calculate the record's position within the file (but extra work is required of the program doing so). Nevertheless, records are usually accessed sequentially. Inserting a record still requires rewriting the file, as the remaining records must shift to accommodate the new record.

There is no key portion of a record, nor are the records required to be in any particular sorted order, as in some definitions of sequential.

Indexed

This type of file encompasses the terms *Indexed* and *indexed sequential* (ISAM), depending on what other operating systems one has used. Each record has one or more *keys*, which indicate the logical sequence of records within the file. For example, an employee's last name or identification number may serve as a key. This allows a given record to be reached quickly and allows insertions of records without rewriting the entire file. Complex pointers are automatically manipulated so that the ordering of records is maintained when inserting and deleting records. When read sequentially, records are automatically read in key order. The previous and next records may also be accessed, relative to the record most recently referenced.

Relative

In relative files, records are of a fixed length and are accessed by record number within the file, starting from the beginning. The system calculates the position of a record from the record size and record number within the file.

This type of access is similar to directly accessing a sequential file with fixed-length records. With a relative file, however, OpenVMS services automatically perform much of the necessary work.

Why Are Programs Stored As Sequential Files?

To highlight the practical similarities of relative files to fixed-record-length sequential files, note that executable images (programs) on OpenVMS are stored as sequential files with a record size of 512 bytes (a size convenient for the OpenVMS virtual memory management subsystem, as well as the size of a disk "block"). Even though program files are sequential, they are typically accessed by block number.

Disk Structure Levels

Some versions of OpenVMS support more than one disk organization. This is similar to a Windows NT system, which supports both the FAT and NTFS disk structures.

Most OpenVMS disks are structured as On-Disk Structure Version 2 (ODS-2) volumes. Some versions of OpenVMS support a newer disk organization, ODS-5.

ODS-5 is intended primarily to provide a disk environment more akin to the environments found on personal computer systems, including Microsoft Windows. ODS-5 supports longer filenames, deeper directory nesting, and a wider variety of legal characters in filenames than does ODS-2. These characteristics make it convenient to serve an ODS-5 volume to computers running different operating systems across the network.

ODS-5 is supported on Alpha beginning with OpenVMS Alpha V7.2 and has limited support on VAX beginning with OpenVMS VAX V7.2. Even so, not all OpenVMS applications directly support ODS-5.

Examples given in this book use ODS-2 filename and directory rules, which will also work under ODS-5.

Components of an ODS-2 File Specification

In order for the system to identify a particular file correctly, each file must have a name that is unique among all files on the network, the operative phrase being "on the network." Two different OpenVMS systems may have disks, directories, and files with identical names, but must be able to tell them apart.

To differentiate among these files, a full file specification is necessary. It contains enough information to identify any given file on the network uniquely.

A full file specification follows this format:

```
NODE::DEVICE:[DIR.SUBDIR1.SUBDIR2(...)]NAME.EXT;VERSION
```

Let's examine each component.

NODE:: is the computer upon which the disk and directory reside. This field is required when only accessing a file or directory on some other computer on the network. It is the nodename of the computer followed by two colons. If the other node requires user authentication, this field takes the form *NODE"username password"::*.

DEVICE: is the disk device on which the directory resides. It ends with a single colon. The standard format for device names is discussed elsewhere in this chapter.

[DIR.SUBDIR1.SUBDIR2] is the directory. Directories are explained in detail in the following section. A directory is contained within brackets ([ ]), and each subdirectory level (if any) is separated by a dot (.). The top-level directory has the format [DIR]. The first subdirectory level is denoted [DIR.SUBDIR1]; the second, [DIR.SUBDIR1.SUBDIR2]; and so forth. Earlier versions of OpenVMS limited subdirectories to a depth of seven, but later versions lift this restriction.

The NAME consists of up to 39 characters that identify the file. On an ODS-2 disk, all alphabetic characters are treated as if they were upper case. They will be stored and displayed in upper case, but you may use any combination of upper and lower-case when identifying the file. Valid characters are letters, numbers, the underscore (_), the dollar sign ($), and the hyphen (-).

EXT stands for extension. This is a 0- to 39-character field that identifies the type of file it is. It is preceded by a dot, which is present even with a zero-length (null) filetype. Legal characters are the same as for the NAME field. You may use any legal characters you wish, but the system automatically assumes some default extensions for various types of files. Examples include .LOG for batch log files, .COM for DCL command procedures, and .EXE for executable programs. See Appendix C for common default filetypes.

VERSION is a number from 1 to 32767 identifying a version number for the file. Version numbers are a feature not found on some other systems. When you create a new file, it is assigned a version number of 1, unless you specify a different number. If you later edit and save the file, version 2 is created, but version 1 continues to exist. This avoids a common problem of some other systems, where saving a file overwrites the old contents. Under OpenVMS, a previous version of a file can be accessed by specifying its version number. Previous versions are deleted with the PURGE command or by an optional version limit which can be different for each file.

Under ODS-2, all fields are case-insensitive. You may use any combination of upper and lower case to specify filenames. The system will display filenames in upper case only.

Differences in ODS-5

OpenVMS Alpha V7.2 and later and presumably OpenVMS Itanium support an additional disk structure: On-Disk Structure Version 5 (ODS-5). ODS-5 supports additional legal characters in filenames and a deeper directory level nesting. These extended filename rules support filenames similar to those found in Microsoft Windows 95/98 and Windows NT.

ODS-5 is provided primarily to support file-sharing capabilities for DCOM and JAVA applications and remote systems supporting file specifications that cannot be directly represented by ODS-2. General users can use ODS-5 volumes, but please be aware that many OpenVMS programs are not guaranteed to work properly with ODS-5 volumes. The number of compatible applications will likely increase over the next few versions of OpenVMS.

OpenVMS VAX Version V7.2 and later include only limited support for ODS-5. While participating in a cluster with an OpenVMS Alpha system, a VAX system may mount an ODS-5 disk, but can process only files that comply with ODS-2 rules.

Filenames under ODS-5 can be up to 236 8-bit characters in length, or 118 16-bit characters. Filenames can contain 8-bit ISO Latin-1 and 16-bit Unicode (UCS-2) characters, except for double quotes (" "), asterisks (*), backslashes (\), colons (:), angle brackets (< >), slashes (/), question marks (?), and vertical bars (|). To enter certain characters unambiguously in a file specification (such as a space), you must precede the character with a circumflex (^). Directory names can support most of the same characters as filenames. Periods and other special characters must be preceded by a circumflex.

ODS-5 file specifications are case-sensitive, and ODS-5 can support up to 255 levels of directory nesting.

See the *OpenVMS Guide to Extended File Specifications* for further information.

Working with Files

The following sections introduce the reader to commonly performed functions related to files. As stated previously, the file is the basic unit of data storage and most operations will involve files in some way.

Displaying a List of Files (the DIRECTORY command)

The DIRECTORY command displays information about one or more files contained in one or more *directories*. Directories are explained in detail later, but for now just be aware that a directory is a grouping of related files. Each user typically has a separate directory to keep his or her files separate from those of other users. Some operating systems use the term folder in place of directory.

DIRECTORY can display the names, sizes, dates of creation, and other details about files, depending on the qualifiers you use. The simplest form of the command shows only the names, types, and versions of files in the current default directory:

```
$ DIRECTORY

Directory DKA100:[MIKE.SCENE]

SCENE.C;1          SCENE.EXE;1          SCENE.OBJ;1

Total of 3 files.
```

The top line of the display indicates that the current directory is DKA100:[MIKE.SCENE] This means that the directory resides on a disk called DKA100:, on which there is a directory called MIKE, and within it, a directory called SCENE. A directory may contain subdirectories; think of such subdirectories as folders within a folder.

In this example directory, there are three files: SCENE.C, SCENE.EXE, and SCENE.OBJ. You will notice that directories automatically maintain files in alphabetical order.

The information shown by the simplest DIRECTORY command is quite basic, displaying only the names of the files. But DIRECTORY has numerous qualifiers that can display detailed information about files. For example, let's say you wish to see the date and time each file was last modified, its size, and its owner. You would use this command:

```
$ DIRECTORY/SIZE/DATE=MODIFIED/OWNER

Directory DKA100:[MIKE.SCENE]

SCENE.C;1                  23    5-NOV-2002 20:47:50.14   [MIKE]
SCENE.EXE;1               128    5-NOV-2002 20:49:02.88   [MIKE]
SCENE.OBJ;1               11     5-NOV-2002 20:48:23.61   [MIKE]

Total of 3 files, 162 blocks.
```

Note: File sizes are shown in 512-byte blocks. SCENE.OBJ is about 5,632 bytes in size.

You may use DIRECTORY to show only certain files by specifying one or more files as parameters:

```
$ DIRECTORY/SECURITY SCENE.OBJ

Directory DKA100:[MIKE.SCENE]

SCENE.OBJ;1              [MIKE]                    (RWED,RWED,RE,)

Total of 1 file.
```

The example above also includes the /SECURITY qualifier, which instructs the DIRECTORY command to show the ownership and file protection of any files displayed.

You may even examine files in another directory by specifying the directory as part of the parameter:

```
$ DIRECTORY [MIKE]*.EXE

Directory DKA100:[MIKE]

DECRYPT.EXE;8        ENCRYPT.EXE;1        FINGER.EXE;1        FIRST.EXE;1
MIKESUMM.EXE;1       MYSTIFY.EXE;3        TEST.EXE;3          UNZIP_AXP.EXE;1
ZIP_AXP.EXE;1

Total of 9 files.
```

You may have noticed that the previous example uses an asterisk (*) in place of part of a filename. This is a *wildcard* character, which means it will match any sequence of characters found at that location in a file specification. The use of wildcards is discussed subsequently.

File Sizes

OpenVMS expresses file sizes in *blocks*. A block is 512 bytes or 0.5KB. The following table shows various sizes expressed as blocks:

```
Bytes     Blocks
512       1
1K        2
25K       50
50K       100
100K      200
500K      1,000
1M        2,048
10M       20,480
100M      204,800
1G        2,097,162
```

File Specification Defaults

A full file specification can become quite long. However, you usually do not need to type all of it; OpenVMS assumes default values for almost all fields within the specification.

Every field from the nodename through directory, if omitted, will default to the current value: current node, current disk, and current directory. The version number, if omitted, will default to the highest version that currently exists. Even the file extension may assume a default value, depending on the context in which the file is referenced. Appendix C contains a listing of common default filetypes.

Let's say I have a command procedure in my home directory whose full file specification is PHOEBE::DKA100:[MIKE]TALLY.COM;34. Assuming my current disk and directory are the same, I can execute it by issuing this simple command:

```
$ @TALLY
```

Wildcards

Wildcards are special characters that match any character (or sequence of characters) in a file specification. You may use them to identify only those files in which you are interested. Wildcard characters may be used in the directory, filename, filetype, and version fields of a file specification. Using them in the node or device fields is not permitted.

> **Note:** Wildcards as used in directory specifications will be discussed later along with directories.

The wildcard characters used to match file specifications are as follows:

- *—The asterisk wildcard character matches zero or more characters at the position in a file specification where it appears.

- %—The percent sign matches exactly one character at the position in a file specification where it appears. Some examples follow.

```
This file specification                 Will match these files

*.DAT                                   JUNIOR.DAT
                                        BRADY.DAT

19*.TXT                                 1996.TXT
                                        19_BOTTLES_OF_BEER.TXT

*USE*.DAT                               USERGUIDE.DAT
                                        SYSTEM_USERS.DAT

TEST.*                                  TEST.C
                                        TEST.EXE

199%.DAT                                1996.DAT
                                        199A.DAT
```

Some commands using wildcards might be:

```
$ DELETE *.TMP;*
```

Deletes all versions of all files in the current directory of the type .TMP.

```
$ TYPE CHAPTER*.TXT
```

Displays the contents of the most recent version of each file in the current directory whose name begins with "chapter" and that is of type .TXT.

```
$ TYPE CHAPTER*.TXT;*
```

Displays the contents of all versions of each file in the current directory whose name begins with "chapter" and that is of type .TXT.

```
$ DIRECTORY CHAPTER2.TXT;-1
```

Finds the previous version of CHAPTER2.TXT. The version ";-1" specifies the previous version, ";-2" specifies the version before that, etc. The notation ";-0" refers to the oldest version in existence. The notation ";" or ";0" specifies the highest version in existence.

Creating a File

To create a text file from scratch, you may use a text editor or use the CREATE command. For most purposes, using a text editor is more convenient than using CREATE.

To use CREATE, enter "CREATE *filespec*" at the DCL prompt. Then, type the contents of your file. Each line you type will be placed into the file. You may fix mistakes on the current line only; once you press ENTER to end a line you may no longer make changes to that line. When finished entering lines, press CTRL/Z. This closes the file and returns you to the DCL prompt.

To create a file with the same contents as an existing file, use the COPY command, described later. You may also use a text editor on an existing file and save it under a different name.

Files other than text files are usually created by a program, not directly by a user, and are not covered here.

Displaying a File

To display the contents of a text file on the screen, use the TYPE command:

```
$ TYPE filespec
```

The contents of the file are displayed on your terminal. Use the /PAGE qualifier to display long files one page at a time. You may use the /TAIL=n qualifier to display the last n lines of a file.

Use caution when trying to TYPE any files that are not ordinary text files. Other types of files (say, executable programs or object files) usually contain sequences of unprintable control characters that cause rapid scrolling and beeping (at best) or may cause your terminal to freeze (at worst). If this happens, you may need to reset your terminal.

Deleting a File

To delete one or more files, use the DELETE command:

```
$ DELETE filespec
```

When deleting files, you must specify a version number or use a wildcard in the version field. Use caution when using wildcards other than in the version field because you may accidentally delete more files than intended.

You may wish to consider using these qualifiers with the DELETE command:

- /CONFIRM — Displays each filespec before deletion and asks you whether you would like to delete it. Affirmative answers (which may be abbreviated) are *yes, true, 1* and *all*. ALL deletes all remaining files without confirming them. Negative answers are *no, false, 0,* and *quit*. QUIT exits the delete command immediately without processing any more files.

- /LOG — Displays the file specification of each file deleted and its size; displays a summary after all files have been processed.

Renaming a File

Files are renamed by using the RENAME command. It has a simple format, as follows:

```
$ RENAME original_name new_name
```

If you exclude a specific version number, the highest version will be renamed, leaving any previous versions intact. Therefore, the previous version becomes the highest version of the original file. To rename all versions of a file, include the asterisk wildcard in the version field of *original_name* (filename.type;*).

You may also use the RENAME command to move a file from one directory to another, so long as it remains on the same disk. Simply include a new directory specification in *new_name*:

```
$ RENAME [REPORTS]FEBRUARY.RPT [OLD_REPORTS]FEBRUARY_2003.RPT
```

RENAME supports the /CONFIRM and /LOG qualifiers just as DELETE does.

Copying a File

Files are copied by using the COPY command:

```
$ COPY original_name new_name
```

As with RENAME, omitting a version number causes only the highest version to be copied. You may also use COPY to combine several files into one by using a plus sign between original files or by using wildcards:

```
$ COPY CAKE.TXT+COOKIES.TXT+FLAN.TXT DESSERTS.TXT
```

or

```
$ COPY DECEMBER*.RPT DECEMBER_ALL.RPT
```

Use this feature only with simple sequential files, and avoid using it with other formats, such as indexed and relative. As usual, this command supports /CONFIRM and /LOG. The original files are not deleted.

Deleting Previous Versions of Files

When you modify an existing file, OpenVMS creates a new version of that file and retains previous versions. In a very short time, a large number of previous versions can accumulate, consuming disk space and making directory listings longer.

You may use the PURGE command to delete previous versions of existing files.

Some examples are as follows.

- To delete all versions of all files in the current directory except the highest version of each file:

    ```
    $ PURGE
    ```

- To delete all previous versions of all files with the .LOG filetype.

    ```
    $ PURGE *.LOG
    ```

- To delete all but the latest five versions of LOGIN.COM:

    ```
    $ PURGE/KEEP=5 LOGIN.COM
    ```

The /KEEP=*n* qualifier instructs PURGE to retain the highest *n* versions of each file processed.

Use /CONFIRM to verify each file to be deleted. Answering YES deletes one version at a time. Use caution when answering ALL: Some versions of OpenVMS purge all versions of that particular file only, prompting you again at the next file; other versions of OpenVMS process all remaining files with no further prompts.

You may use /LOG to show you each file deleted and provide a summary after all files have been processed.

Setting File Version Limits

There is another way to control the accumulation of multiple file versions: you may set a version limit for any file. Let's say you set a version limit of five on a particular file. When you create the sixth version of that file, the lowest version will automatically be purged.

If you set a version limit on a file, but a greater number of versions already exists, OpenVMS will not purge files to correct the difference. It will still purge one version for each version created. You must manually purge the extra versions.

You should generally avoid setting a version limit of one; this can occasionally cause problems with some applications that read a previous version in order to create the next version. A minimum value of two is recommended.

To set a version limit of six on a given file:

```
$ SET FILE filespec /VERSION_LIMIT=6
```

Use a value of zero to disable version limits.

If you wish to set an automatic version limit for all future files in a given directory, you may set a default version limit for the directory (see "Using Directories" below). This setting takes effect only for files created after the limit is set. Once set, you may override this value on a per-file basis by using SET FILE/VERSION_LIMIT for any file.

```
$ SET DIRECTORY DKA100:[MIKE]/VERSION_LIMIT=5
```

Again, use a value of zero to disable version limits.

Running a Program

Under OpenVMS, programs have the filetype .EXE. How you run them depends on the expectations of the program. Some programs are part of OpenVMS, and these generally execute automatically in response to the appropriate DCL command. Other programs, such as those you may create yourself with a language compiler or third-party software, may be invoked in different ways.

Other than normal DCL commands that execute standard system programs, there are three main ways to run a program under OpenVMS. They are the *RUN* command, foreign commands, and custom DCL verbs created by the command definition utility (CDU).

The RUN Command

The DCL RUN command is usually used to execute a program that does not need command line arguments. Its format is as follows:

```
$ RUN program_filespec
```

To execute the program COLLECT.EXE in the current directory, use this command:

```
$ RUN COLLECT
```

Note: The RUN command may also be used to start a program running as a detached process (RUN/DETACH). Creating and running such programs is not covered in this book.

Foreign Commands

Native OpenVMS programs often make use of the extensive command line processing capabilities in DCL. However, some programs are written to process their own command lines, such as programs ported from UNIX or some other operating system. For these, a foreign command is usually used.

A foreign command is a special DCL symbol that runs a program and passes the command line directly to the program. Foreign commands may also be used with many programs that do not require command line arguments as an alternative to the RUN command.

Say your program TALLY.EXE should process its own command line. You would create a foreign symbol TALLY as follows:

```
$ TALLY :== $DKB400:[ALICE]TALLY
```

The dollar sign ($) just before the program's file specification is what indicates a foreign command. If you omit the disk and directory, the directory SYS$SYSTEM will be assumed.

Using the symbol TALLY as a command verb will invoke TALLY.EXE and pass the rest of the command line to it. The format of the command line parameters and switches (qualifiers) depends entirely on what TALLY.EXE expects; DCL simply passes the command line to the program. Thus, a program ported from UNIX might have a command line that looks something like this:

```
$ TALLY +iFILE1.DAT +oFILE2.DAT +v+x
```

The above command line will be passed to the program intact, leaving TALLY.EXE to process parameters and switches on its own.

DCL Paths

Later versions of OpenVMS include a way to automatically support foreign commands for executable files residing in a set of directories you define.

Ordinarily, when you enter a command verb that does not match a DCL command, you would receive an error message. With DCL paths, directories of your choice will first be searched for programs with that name. If a matching program is found, it will be invoked as a foreign command.

To define a path search list, define the logical name DCL$PATH, specifying a directory or list of directories to be searched:

```
$ DEFINE DCL$PATH DKA100:[MIKE]
```

or

```
$ DEFINE DCL$PATH DKA100:[MIKE.TOOLS],DKA0:[UTILITIES]
```

Note: logical names are described further on in this chapter.

Let's say that a program DKA0:[UTILITIES]ENCRYPT.EXE exists. Once the DCL path has been defined, you can use ENCRYPT as a command verb, and DCL will automatically locate the program and invoke it as a foreign command.

Custom DCL Commands

When a programmer writes a program specifically designed for OpenVMS, the programmer may elect to take advantage of the extensive command line capabilities of DCL using the OpenVMS CDU. Using this feature, new DCL verbs, along with qualifiers, keywords, and parameters can be created.

Digital, Compaq, and Hewlett-Packard software products, third-party software products, or programs developed by end users may use this feature. Many sites include these custom commands in the system wide DCL command tables, making them available to all users. In fact, you may never become aware that some of the commands you use on a daily basis may have been added to your system in just this way.

Your system manager may notify you about any custom commands available to you, as well as any additional steps you must take to use them.

The material in Appendix A is drawn from Chapter 7 of Michael D. Duffy, *Getting Started with OpenVMS: A Guide for New Users*, 1-55558-279-6, 2002, © Elsevier Science (USA).

Appendix B — VMS and the Web

By Alan Winston

In a way, this chapter also answers the question "Why VMS?" A short answer is "Because it was there from the start."

Beginnings

As you may well recall, Tim Bernars-Lee at CERN, the European high- energy physics laboratory, invented the Web as a convenient means of sharing high-energy physics information stored in different forms on diverse servers. VMS systems were big players in the scientific community. (They'd been preeminent in the middle 1980s, but the price/performance of RISC-based UNIX workstations compared with that of the VAXes, which were the only VMS platform at the time, meant that the price-sensitive and performance-hungry scientific market was buying a lot of those as well.) So CERN developed Web servers for UNIX, for IBM machines, and for VMS.

The Web uses the HyperText Transfer Protocol (HTTP), so a typical name for a Web server is HTTPd, with the "d" standing for "daemon." (A "daemon"—an essential concept on UNIX systems—is a program that runs in the background, listening until it recognizes that it needs to do something, then doing it.) The first HTTPd was developed at CERN; and the first non-European Web server was installed at SLAC[1] in December 1991 (running on an IBM mainframe). My site started running the CERN HTTP server on VMS in 1993 (on a VAX 8700).

A basic Web server, one that just takes requests and serves files, isn't that hard to write. The requirements begin to get exponentially more complicated when the server needs to provide dynamic content in various ways; when it needs to support encrypted communication; when it needs to handle heavy loads gracefully; and when it needs to be robust and secure in the face of hacking attempts and badly behaved browser software. The Web actually started before the Internet went commercial, and the environment for Web servers changed considerably when that happened.

CERN eventually needed to spend its money on the Large Hadron Collider and ceased WWW software development after December 1994. (The CERN server can still be found on the OpenVMS Freeware CD.) Various computer science and physics sites had already developed browsers, including SLAC; the National Center for Supercomputing Applications had already developed Mosaic (whose developers went on to found Netscape) and produced an NCSA HTTPd; but development on that product stopped when the primary author, Rob McCool, left. NCSA HTTPd was the most popular server on the Web, but Webmasters now had to develop their own

---

1. www.slac.stanford.edu

patches, changes, fixes, and enhancements without any coordination, and the program was wandering in different directions.

OSU

In 1994 came the first release of an excellent freeware server on VMS, which I have used at my site since 1995: the Ohio State University DECthreads HTTP server (OSU) written by David Jones. It has been actively enhanced and maintained ever since.

Apache

In February 1995, a group of Webmasters "got together" via mailing list to support the NCSA HTTPd product. They combined their patches and bug fixes, and by April 1995 they made the first official public release of the Apache server (version 0.6.2). Because of all the patches, it was "a patchy server"—I'm afraid that's where the name came from.

The Webmasters developed a methodology for making changes to the core, a method of "lazy consensus," in which no changes could be checked into the archive without a number of "Yes" votes and an absence of "No" votes. You got voting rights by being recognized as a useful contributor to Apache development.

Using this methodology for working together, the Apache group started improving the server. Version 0.7 involved various new features, but version 0.8 had a new server architecture incorporating features for speed (e.g., spinning off new processes before they were needed) and extensibility (e.g., a clearly defined application programming interface [API] and a modular structure). After lots more work, Apache version 1.0 came out in December 1995, extensively tested, ported to lots of UNIX platforms, and adequately documented. Within a year, it was the most popular server on the Web, and it has held that leadership position since. Some 6 million sites run Apache, including Amazon.com, Hewlett-Packard, the *Financial Times*, and the English royal family (www.royal.gov.uk).

Apache runs on Linux, FreeBSD, on other UNIX variants, on Windows NT, MacOS X, OS/2, and now on OpenVMS. Compaq, VMS's proprietor at the time, created the Apache port. The current version is CSWS 1.2 (based on Apache 1.3.20, mod_ssl 2.8.4, and OpenSSL 0.9.5a). The CSWS engineers are working with the Apache Software Foundation to get their port checked in to the official CVS repository.

Apache 2.0, currently in test, is a rewritten server organized with the platform-specific services isolated in the Apache run-time library (APR) and multiprocessing modules (MPM). The rest of the code is platform-independent. This should considerably simplify the process of porting 2.0 for a later release of CSWS.

WASD and others

In 1995 came the release of Process Software's Purveyor, a commercial Web server for VMS. Support was dropped in 1999. (It can still be purchased on an "as-is" basis or downloaded and run for free by hobbyists, but source code is not available.) At this writing, the Multinet Web site[1] is still running Purveyor, and Compaq's own site[2] didn't switch from Purveyor to Apache until September 2001. This book doesn't cover Purveyor because it's unsupported and not under active development; for the same reason I don't cover the port of Netscape FastTrack Server to VMS. (The retirement and end-of-support date for FastTrack is December 31, 2001, on OpenVMS Alpha V7.1-2 and June 30, 2002, for OpenVMS Alpha V7.2-1 and V7.2-2.) Also in 1995, TGV (the company that originated Multinet) produced the Cheetah Web server but dropped it in 1997. VMS was not proving a profitable market for commercial Web server software. It's not entirely clear that a profitable market for Web server software exists anywhere, with the ubiquitous availability of free alternatives. (I would have said "free high-quality alternatives," but that wouldn't have covered IIS.) Figure B-1 illustrates the Web server timeline.

In 1996 Mark Daniel in Australia came out with the first public release of the WASD (initially HFRD) server, which had been working inside the High Frequency Radar Division of the Defense Science and Technology Organization for some 18 months before that. Both OSU and WASD were adopted fairly widely and have grown user communities; both are still under active development.

Web Options

At this stage in history, the real options for VMS Web serving are CSWS/Apache, OSU, and WASD. (There are still some vocal adherents of Purveyor from Process Software, but it doesn't really make much sense to start any new project on a server

1991	1993	1994	1995	1996	1997	1998	1999	2000
First Web server at CERN—runs on IBM, UNIX, VMS First North American Web site at SLAC (on IBM-VM)	My site adopts CERN server on VMS	CERN server no longer supported on VMS NCSA Server released grows into Apache OSU Server version 1 released.	Purveyor released on VMS Cheetah released on VMS Apache 1.0	HFRD Server (later WASD) released.	Cheetah is dropped	Netscape FastTrack Server on VMS	Purveyor no longer supported	CSWS/Apache 1.0 on VMS.

Figure B-1 Web server timeline.

1. multinet.process.com
2. www.openvms.compaq.com

that's neither Open Source nor supported, no matter how solidly it works.) Here's an overview of what the three programs offer.

CSWS

Compaq Secure Web Server (CSWS) is an official, Compaq-supported port of Apache, the most popular Web server on the planet. It's available for download from the OpenVMS Web page (www.openvms.compaq.com/openvms/products/ips/apache/csws.html). If you have a support contract for VMS, you have support for Apache, so you can call in if you find bugs. It comes as a PCSI kit and is extremely easy to install, delivering compiled images that are ready to go, so you don't need to have a C compiler on your system. (I will endeavor to use "CSWS" when referring to the VMS port in particular, and "Apache" for how Apache generally works.)

The most widely used add-ons for Apache are probably mod_ssl, FrontPage extensions, mod_php, and mod_perl. Compaq has ported mod_ssl and mod_perl, created a supported port of Perl, created a new module for OpenVMS user authorization, added a module that lets you run CGI programs written for the OSU Web server, added mod_php in the 1.2 beta release, and added mod_rewrite as well. There are dozens of modules available for Apache on other platforms; it's hoped that a VMS community will develop around Apache/CSWS and port more of the modules. (I'd certainly like to see mod_python, since there's a VMS port of that scripting language. There was a port of mod_python for an early version of Python.) There is at present no port of the FrontPage extensions to VMS. Mod_include, the server-side include module, is part of the core, so CSWS can do very full server-side includes that incorporate some scripting logic. CSWS can run Java servlets (if Java's installed), and Compaq also makes Tomcat/Jakarta, the Java application server, available on VMS. (Jakarta won't be discussed in much detail in this book.)

Perl is the amazingly capable scripting/glue language that, in addition to a lot of data manipulation and system management applications, turned out to be perfect for Web programming through the Common Gateway Interface. mod_perl embeds a persistent copy of the Perl interpreter into Apache, with two good effects: When the server needs to process a Perl script, it doesn't have to spend the time to fire up a separate process and load Perl from disk. It can handle the request faster and with less overall system load. In addition, it means that Apache can be extended with Perl modules, instead of being limited to writing, compiling, and linking additional C modules. (The mod_perl interface exposes enough of the Apache internal state to Perl that Perl modules can be involved in Apache's internal processing.)

A Perl module such as Apache::ASP brings Active Server Pages functionality, developed for Microsoft's IIS, to Perl. mod_perl in CSWS 1.1 works only with the version of Perl it was built with (5.5.3), which is not the most up-to-date version; still, with some ingenuity you can use later versions of Perl in CGI scripts but not with mod_perl. The CSW 1.2 has a CSWS_PERL and mod_perl that use Perl 5.6.1, which is the most current stable Perl version as this is written, although Perl development continues apace. See Appendix A for more about Perl history and capability. PHP is the PHP HyperText Processor, the most popular Web-templating language; see Appendix C for more about PHP's history and capability.

There are more add-ons and modules for Apache than for any other Web server, but they aren't supported by Compaq. Just because something runs on UNIX or Windows Apache doesn't mean it will necessarily work on VMS at all or without considerable porting effort, but it will probably be easier to get something that exists working than to build something from scratch. Some things that are fairly standard on UNIX Apaches (e.g., using the Berkeley database manager for authentication files) aren't supported on VMS; I'll point these instances out as we come to them.

The VMS Apache port runs only on Alpha, not on VAX. It requires VMS 7.2-1 or higher. In order to maximize portability, the port doesn't radically change the Apache core very much. As a result, it doesn't really take advantage of many of VMS's unique features—exceptions include that processes use shared memory to communicate rather than keeping a scoreboard file on disk and the use of Galactic shared memory for SSL session cache—and doesn't wring out the last possible bit of performance from the hardware.

CSWS doesn't offer a Web-based administration tool. (There are a number of third-party add-ons that do this on UNIX.) Most configuration will be done by editing the configuration file.

OSU

The Ohio State University DECthreads HTTP Server, developed by David Jones, is available from http://kcgl1.eng.ohio-state.edu/www/doc/serverinfo.html. Jones also wrote a freeware secure shell server for VMS, the first available SSH server on VMS as far as I know. (Multinet and TCPware include SSH servers, but TCP/IP Services doesn't offer one, and no plans to offer one have been announced so far.)

You can get OSU to run on VAX or Alpha with any version from 5.5-2 on up. (For versions of VMS higher than 7.2 you need to run OSU 3.6b or higher. The current version as of this writing is OSU 3.9b, with 3.10alpha in alpha test.) OSU uses threading to handle concurrent Web requests. If you're running a multiprocessor box and a version of VMS recent enough to handle kernel threads properly, you can take advantage of your CPU investment by automatically running different threads from the same image concurrently on any available processor. (OSU is really good at exposing bugs in VMS's threading implementation, and you may need to turn off kernel threading in the server. Also, the threading model has changed a couple of times, so if you're on an old-enough VMS version you may need to run an old version of OSU.)

To communicate with CGI worker processes, OSU uses DECnet internally—that is, without going outside the server box. (There's a hack that uses VMS mailboxes instead, but that isn't in common use and is really intended only for testing.) Because of the DECnet method, the scripting environment isn't completely standard, and scripts developed for other Web servers often need a small DCL wrapper to work properly. (An exception is made for Perl scripts; the environment sends the right stuff out on the DECnet link and makes the necessary assignments before invoking Perl.) OSU has some support for persistent scripting environments, ranging from using DECnet tweaking to keep the script processes around a long time to a special Webperl image to a High-Performance Script Server process pool manager that accelerates compiled programs linked with the HPSS shareable image. This server can run Java servlets on an Alpha with Java installed. OSU has also has very capable and flexible authentication and access control options.

OSU has no built-in SSL support; you have to build OpenSSL and then create an SSL_ENGINE or SSL_TASK process that communicates with OSU over DECnet, such as a CGI. You definitely need a C compiler if you're going to have encrypted communication support for OSU, and it's a good idea to have one anyway, as there are enough combinations of operating system levels and VMS TCP/IP products that it may be difficult to find a precompiled version of OSU with everything you need.

OSU has very configurable and sophisticated file caching, which gives it an advantage over serving pages just from disk. Some MicroVAX systems serve hundreds of thousands of pages a month, and the cache can help considerably in reducing the system load. Pulling something from memory is a lot cheaper than pulling it from disk.

Documentation is somewhat sketchy. There are example configuration files and some on-line documentation of what they mean, and some users have put up documentation Web pages. Digital Press expects to release an OSU manual in 2002. Quite a lot of server configuration can be done via a Web form, although I prefer editing the configuration files, and most of my examples will be in the form of edited configuration files.

Support is by volunteer effort on the VMS-WEB-DAEMON mailing list. If you have a question or problem, you can raise it on the list and will often get an answer back very promptly, day or night. (Some of the contributors are on different continents, so there's effectively 24-hour coverage.) Jones himself reads the list and answers questions when he's available. I've been using OSU since 1994 and have generally been very happy with it.

WASD

Mark Daniel developed WASD (then HFRD) for internal use at the High Frequency Radar Division of the Defense Science and Technology Organization, and it was in use for some 18 months before being released to the public. The High Frequency Radar Division of the Defense Science and Technology Organization changed its name to Wide Area Surveillance Division, so the package became WASD; later the division became Surveillance Systems Division, but WASD was too well known to change to SSD, and it might have been too easily confused with the secure shell daemon (SSHD). It's available from http://wasd.vsm.com.au. WASD runs on VAX or Alpha.

The idea with WASD was to be a really good VMS-only server; Mark Daniel says, "I suffered a bit of a VMS cringe when amongst my UNIX colleagues (VMS was and is perceived to be a bit slow and cumbersome), so I have also endeavored to make WASD as fast and efficient as I could, avoiding C run-time library and even RMS code layers where it was feasible and worth it. I also wanted a similarly tight scripting environment and have spent a lot of time honing this aspect."

Although everybody's usage varies, WASD seems to be the fastest server available, getting as much performance as possible from the system. WASD supports a number of scripting environments: standard CGI; CGIplus (each with callouts that can request the server to perform certain functions for the CGI and then resume processing); ISAPI (the fast application program interface developed for Microsoft's IIS); a framework for a persistent run-time environment that you can customize to make your own application permanently available, and a Perl processor that takes advantage of this; plus a CGIUTL utility that simplifies the job of DCL scripts. All of these goodies are supplied with object code, but for customization you'll need a C compiler. There's support for Java servlets on Alpha with Java installed, and there's also an OSU compatibility mode. WASD also allows the execution of DCL commands from within server-side include statements in HTML code.

WASD offers server administration and some statistics via a Web form, or you can edit the configuration file manually. To get SSL working you install a separate kit, which includes the OpenSSL object libraries into the WASD directory tree, and then run a script to link. You don't need to make any source code changes. It is also possible to link WASD against the object libraries of an existing OpenSSL installation. This is easier than OSU but marginally harder than CSWS.

Which should you use?

The answer to the question "Which should I use?" is always "It depends." If you're running on a VAX, CSWS isn't an option, so you'll need to choose between OSU and WASD. If your Webmaster already understands Apache, use CSWS. If you need to squeeze out the last bit of performance, use WASD. If your site policies won't let you use software without a support contract, use CSWS (or go to a third-party provider of

OSU or WASD support). If you're not afraid of compiling source code and want a very stable server with a knowledgeable user base, use OSU. If being "industry standard" matters to you—being able to buy O'Reilly handbooks, *Dummy's Guides*, and so on—go with CSWS, but be prepared to find out that the stuff they document isn't in the VMS version, or at least be prepared to have to figure out file names and the like. If you don't have a C compiler, don't use OSU. If you're stuck on a less-current version of VMS (such as the very stable 6.2 or 6.2-1H1), Apache is out of the picture.

In most cases, everything will matter somewhat to you, so you're going to have to prioritize (i.e., figure out what matters most or how much to weight each factor). All of these servers are available for free, so you do have the comforting option of downloading each one and trying it out, seeing how well it works in your environment, and finding out which one you find most congenial to maintain. You can even run them all at once, on different TCP/IP ports, serving the same or different documents.

The material in Appendix B is drawn from Chapters 2 and 3 of Alan Winston, *OpenVMS with Apache, OSU, and WASD: The Nonstop Webserver*, 1-55558-264-8, 2002, © Alan Winston.

Appendix C — Assessing OpenVMS and Linux: The Right Tool for the Right Job

By John Robert Wisniewski

Good, Better, Best

Welcome to the book that answers the questions why OpenVMS? Linux? and just how do you get these two computer operating systems (OSs) to work together?

Why in the world would you want to have them work together? Let me try to answer that by briefly saying that there are customers who adore OpenVMS—its cluster technology and full-service support. Linux is into Open Source, with tens of thousands of coders in its court. What a wild duet! But still, they're cousins—open systems cousins.

Now, without singing the rest of the Patty Duke theme music; the two operating systems have much in common: their network interface protocols; Open Source tools; industry standards; commercial database products; X Windows; and industry-standard security tools for encryption, tunneling, and secure communications. If general tools are on both Linux and OpenVMS, why continue to use two different OSs? Simply because OpenVMS has features and abilities that Linux or any other OS would be hard pressed to deliver.

What does OpenVMS have? OpenVMS provides something that you only get with 25 years of testing and use—enterprise-class stability and reliability in almost every configuration it's used in.

What does Linux bring to the table? Today Linux is Open Source, with thousands of programmers working on new and exciting applications worldwide, sharing base source codes, and delivering low-cost tools and software that improve the entire software industry.

Together, OpenVMS and Linux provide the best of Open Source and the best of commerical applications, giving users a choice about how to deploy various computing styles: client/server, multitiered database servers, or large transaction processing environments.

Between the high end and the low end of computing, various demployment strategies are needed today and will be needed in the future. The line between OpenVMS and Linux deployment decisions should be drawn wherever it needs to be.

Solution architects and system analysts need to understand the best features of both operating systems, as well as their realistic limits, and then measure the actual cost of deployment of Linux and OpenVMS systems, utilizing the best tools for the system or work at hand. OpenVMS can run on workstations to mainframes. Linux runs on mainframes to workstations, drawing a hard line in the sand that limits what will be deployed and limits the types of deployment an organization can deliver. Why not use the best of both worlds to solve computing problems? I know I do!

Why OpenVMS?

After 25 years in a constantly changing computer industry—spanning the PC revolution, DEC becoming Digital, VMS becoming OpenVMS, Compaq buying out Digital, HP buying out Compaq, and OpenVMS migrating from VAX 32-bit CPUs to Alpha 64-bit CPUs, as well as HP's migrating from OpenVMS to IA64 Intel's 64-bit CPU, and the advent of Microsoft products, Open Source and Linux products, UNIX products, the IBM pantheon of operating systems, and fault-tolerant products such as NSK—an industry watcher and career participant has to ask the following question: Why should companies use OpenVMS over the next 5 to 10 years? Considering that OpenVMS has the lowest cost of deployment and maintenance in the industry today, you might ask, why wouldn't you use OpenVMS? Lowest cost is one factor, but technology decisions seem to drive many deployment decisions. Let's review OpenVMS's current abilities.

- *Clustering*: OpenVMS has had the acknowledged best clusters and scaling in the industry since 1983. Its features include single system disk, single unified file system view across all cluster members (even with multiple file systems), shared tapes, shared disks, and up to 96 clustered member systems of desktop to mainframe-size systems, with as many as 32 SMP CPUs each and as much as 10 Tbytes of main memory (RAM) in the entire cluster. All systems are managed as a single system and a single work domain. OpenVMS clusters work out of the box across Ethernet, SANs, and high-speed memory channel connections, with minimal configuration and setup. You can literally add a new member system to an OpenVMS cluster in as little as five minutes (once the hardware has been plugged in).

- *Disaster-Tolerant Clusters*: Data centers can be completely duplicated (all disks, all resources, all transactions) in an active-active cluster at distances of up to 540 miles apart. (Note: Everyone else just offers a hot/warm or hot/cold site technology; OpenVMS uses both sites in an active-active configuration, which uses much less hardware then other active-passive cluster configurations—up to 50 percent less!)

- *Oracle 8*: This deploys larger, runs better, and runs faster on OpenVMS clusters. Oracle RdB continues to be one of the fastest databases in the world, fully integrated into OpenVMS and OpenVMS clusters, with new customers every year.

- *Timeshare*: As the Internet continues to grow and server consolidation continues, systems will be measured by their ability to handle many, many small jobs in a predictable time slot while sharing resources evenly. OpenVMS and its scheduler have been providing and polishing predictable, even real-time, performance since the 1970s. With today's Web server, transaction-servers, and application-server requirements, capacity planning and predictable response for every job is already becoming a prerequisite for deploying even a prototype application.

- *Security*: OpenVMS/VMS has had less then 45 CERT security advisories in the last 13 years. (Windows 2000, 484; Linux, 546; Solaris, 490; AIX, 377 as of June 2002; http://www.cert.org/).

  Deploying other servers in your production environment, you will spend considerably more system-management dollars securing your servers and making sure all the CERT advisories are all plugged than you would if you just deployed OpenVMS out of the box! If you checked all the CERT advisories, it could take hundreds of hours just to review various security holes in other operating systems.

  Out-of-the-box OpenVMS is virtually unhackable (or so say the goons/judges from the DEFCON 9 Hacker Convention, July 2001 http://www.dfwcug.org/dfwcug_newsletters/20107.PDF).

  Kevin Mitnick, celebrity hacker, just testified before Congress that he was defeated for the first time in his life when he recently tried to break into an OpenVMS system in England (http://www.zdnet.com/zdnn/stories/news/0,4586,2454737,00.html).

- *Diicoe*: Defense Information Infrastructure Common Operating Environment certification means that Compaq/HP has signed (in 2001) an agreement with the U.S. government to support OpenVMS for the next 20 years. This allows HP to continue selling OpenVMS to the U.S. government (one of OpenVMS's largest user bases), and it must maintain support for the next 20 years on products sold to the U.S. government.

- *Shared File Systems*: OpenVMS offers integration with Windows 2000 and NT 4.0 SMB file systems via Advanced Server (code from Microsoft). From the

Open Systems (UNIX) side of the house, OpenVMS integrates with NFS (V3.0). OpenVMS can also offer a single directory, which is viewed, coordinated, and accessed by both Windows systems and UNIX systems at the same time!

- *E-business Infrastructure*: Attunity's XML and database gateways are included with the OpenVMS license. Apache, SSH, Java, Microsoft's COM (object-calling standard), CORBA (Open Systems object-calling standard), DCE, and X Windows are all included with OpenVMS with the base license.

- *Service and Support*: For a business that deploys an OS for years at a time, support for past products and previous versions of the OS is critical. HP and OpenVMS continue to support VAX systems (even though they haven't shipped a new VAX in almost 2 years!), and they support previous stable versions of the OpenVMS operating systems as far back as 10 years for customers. It's hard to imagine a 10-year deployment of our latest PC of the hour. Businesses don't enjoy changing applications that are working, and OpenVMS applications, once up and running, tend not to get taken off line, which is one of OpenVMS's most famous hallmarks.

- *High Availablity*: Many companies choose OpenVMS because it's one of the few operating systems that can deliver on its claim of 99.99999 percent (about three minutes downtime per year). If OpenVMS had just started claiming this feat, it might be suspect; but customers have been getting this much service from their machines since the early 1990s (in a properly configured and maintained VMS cluster). Rolling upgrades of software and the OS, and continuous processing for years at a time, are other milestones that OpenVMS pioneered.

After 25 years as a computer, application, and database server, very few of the other operating systems can even begin to match OpenVMS as a deployment platform. While OpenVMS will never be the best games desktop, it has already proven itself the finest, most robust, most secure, and most clusterable OS in our industry today. But wait: Don't touch that dial, there's more! If OpenVMS were just another OS with the most features in our industry, that might be good enough; but what would you pay for such a fantastic tool? Two times or four times the cost of an average UNIX server? How about if OpenVMS gave you all this capability and had the lowest cost of ownership in the industry compared with all other UNIX systems and mainframes? Well, don't believe me—check out the study Techwise Research did on OpenVMS in 2001, where they found that OpenVMS had the lowest cost of ownership of any server deployment over a five year period (http://www.openvms.compaq.com/openvms/whitepapers/techwise.html).

Tested and supported features, lowest cost of ownership and deployment in the industry, highest availability and scalability, and a 25-year track record with interoperability with all the latest Internet and e-business software and tools—that's why you will use OpenVMS for the next 10 years.

Why Linux?

When Linus Torval started his project, he dreamed of an OS unencumbered by source-code restrictions and copyrights. In just a few short years, Linux workstations and servers began to emerge as a powerful Open Source alternative to Windows desktops and many UNIX servers. Productivity tools such as Star Office, WordPerfect, and many other application ports were available. Games were also available on these strange new Open Source boxes. As the desktop functionality grew, many saw computer server functions as Linux's destiny. Linux is a workstation and a server with a graphical user interface for management (Gnome and KDE are the two interfaces of choice). With HP and others beginning to offer certification as Linux Accredited Systems Engineers, support and services are beginning to mature.

So where does Linux fit in today's IT strategy? Let's review some of its features.

- *Laptop*: With Sun's Star Office or Corel's WordPerfect 2000 suite, a Linux installation offers the users less disk space consumption than a comparable Windows OS and Office suite. Linux also offers the ability to reuse two-to-three- year-old laptops that are now too underpowered to run the latest versions of Windows products, but it can also run the latest versions of Linux and many personal productivity tools that run on the platform. For Microsoft interoperability Bynari Systems also offers bug-for-bug compatibility with Windows Exchange Clients (Outlook) and Windows-compatible Exchange Servers for Linux and UNIX systems to integrate directly into Exchange E-mail Server infrastructures. Alternatively, Linux and other TCP/IP users can use Netscape mail, if they have POP3 or IMAP servers already in place (http://www.bynari.com/, http://www.sun.com/staroffice/, http://linux.corel.com/).

- *Workstation*: What goes for laptops goes even more so for Linux desktops. A few-year-old 300–500MHz Pentium workstation or even Alpha workstation can run Linux and its applications blazingly fast. Instead of buying new workstations with 50 percent more memory and disk space, recycling a used desktop saves money and upgrades easily to Linux with as much ease of use as Windows desktops. And while there have been some demands for enhanced Linux security, it's nothing like the defense that must be mounted against the

65,000+ virus definitions that Windows programs must be defended against every day when on a public network.

- *X Window Terminal*: Linux workstations and laptops make excellent X Windows display terminals. Linux, UNIX, and OpenVMS all use X Windows and various X Windows managers and programs to redirect output to remote machines across Ethernet or other network connections. Today, Microsoft Windows has programs to perform X Server displays, but Linux has built-in X Windows security and the same X Windows features as its larger UNIX and OpenVMS cousins. Therefore, bringing all your OpenVMS and UNIX application displays down from a headless server to a single, low-cost, high-quality desktop with a great choice of graphics and sound cards is a wonderful alternative to purchasing expensive workstations. (Although, just like driving a Ferrari, once you've worked on a full-blown 64-bit UNIX or VMS workstation, it's hard to go back—no matter how "sporty" the 32-bit Chevy becomes.)

- *Server*: As a bottom-tier server (in the standard three-tier client/server model), Linux is as good or better then any single NT, UNIX or OpenVMS server. Linux servers support SAMBA for disk shares with Windows servers and clients, NFS for disk mount points for UNIX and OpenVMS machines, Java, Apache, and all the major computer languages and scripting tools. The problem is that Linux servers no matter how functional, live within mean time between failures of their hardware. Sooner or later a deployed single server will have a failure that takes out critical data or programs, and then the system will have to be restored or rebuilt. Commercial clustering for Linux servers is in its infancy, as are automatic failover environments for Linux. As support, cluster technology, and shared storage (SAN, networked storage) continue to mature, so will the use of Linux servers for data-center applications.

The Bottom Line

OpenVMS systems and Linux systems have much in common with UNIX and Windows servers, with some distinct advantages for each. Given our heterogeneous computing environments of today and looking toward the future, both OpenVMS and Linux will find a use in our data centers and professional information services (IS) deployments for many years to come—OpenVMS for its high availability and scalability and Linux for its low per-unit cost structure and its huge Open Source libraries of software.

As we move forward in this millennium, the battle cry should be for the lowest-cost, right tool for every style of computing. Between OpenVMS and Linux operating systems, a very large part of the computing spectrum is being delivered, and in a most cost-effective way. Now let's explore the types of things both Linux and OpenVMS can do together!

The rest of the chapters in this book are a series of how-to processes designed to utilize both your OpenVMS and Linux box in different ways (TCP/IP, NFS, E-mail, X Windows, and more). The procedures are easy and to the point. They should also be a good starting point for you to explore these functions for more advanced use and deployment! You won't need to read this book cover to cover; the chapters should be self-contained and, I hope, a good reference for some of your specific Linux and OpenVMS interoperability issues.

The rest of this book assumes that you have a running OpenVMS and Linux system configured with TCP/IP and a working knowledge of both OSs as a user and operator. You'll also need system privileges on both systems; don't worry, Chapter 2 shows you how to get System and root on your boxes. But don't experiment on your production machines; two small workstations in the same network would be a great test bed as you learn to connect OpenVMS and Linux together.

The material in Appendix C is drawn from Chapter 1 of John Robert Wisniewski, *Linux and OpenVMS Interoperability: Tricks for Old Dogs, New Dogs, and Hot Dogs with Open Systems*, 2003, 1-55558-267-2, Copyright © 2003 Hewlett-Packard Development Company, L.P.

Appendix D — Memory Management System Services

By Ruth E. Goldenberg

A place for everything and everything in its place.
Isabella Mary Beeton, The Book of Household Management

This appendix describes those system services that affect process-private virtual address space and several related others:

- $CREATE_REGION_64, which assigns characteristics to an area of a given size

- $CRETVA and $CRETVA_64, which create demand zero pages in P0, P1, and P2 space

- $EXPREG and $EXPREG_64, which create demand zero pages at the next available address within a specified virtual address region

- Various create and map section services that create a process-private or global section that maps the blocks of a file or particular pages of physical address space to a portion of process-private address space

- Various create and map section services that create and map memory-resident or Galaxywide global sections

- $MGBLSC, $MGBLSC_64, and $MGBLSC_GPFN_64, which map to an existing global section

- $DELTVA and $DELTVA_64, which delete P0, P1, or P2 pages

- $CNTREG, which deletes the upper end of P0 space or the lower end of P1 space

- $DGBLSC, which marks a global section for deletion when no more processes are mapped to it

- $DELETE_REGION_64, which deletes a given region

- $CREATE_BUFOBJ and $CREATE_BUFOBJ_64, which create a buffer object

- $DELETE_BUFOBJ, which deletes a buffer object

- Services that return information about address space, such as $GET_REGION_ INFO, $GETSECI, and $FIND_GPAGE_64

- $SETSWM, which enables or disables process swapping

- $SETPRT and $SETPRT_64, which change the protection on pages of virtual address space

- $SETFLT and $SETFLT_64, which set the fault-on-execute bit for a page

- $COPY_FOR_PAGE, which reads data from a page with fault-on-read set

Common Characteristics of Memory Management System Services

This appendix describes several types of memory management system services. The original system services accept only 32-bit address arguments and have been supplemented with 64-bit services that take 64-bit address arguments. The latter have names ending in _64 to indicate that they accept 64-bit addresses by reference. For example, $CRETVA is the original system service requested to create virtual address space. It continues to be used, but to create P2 space, an application must request $CRETVA_64. This appendix uses the term 32-bit services to refer to the original services and the term 64-bit services for the services whose names end in _64 or services that can affect P2 space.

When 64-bit support was provided for $CRMPSC, that complex system service was split into a number of new services. $CRMPSC both creates and maps various types of process and global sections. The new services deal with either process or global sections, but not both. Generally, three new services are provided for each type of section: one to create the section if it does not already exist and then to map it, one simply to create the section, and one simply to map an existing section. The names of many of the new services end in _64, for example, $CRMPSC_PFN_64, but those without address arguments do not, for example, $CREATE_GPFN.

A process's ability to use the services described in this appendix may be limited by access mode, process quotas, limits, privileges, and SYSGEN parameters.

The level 3 page table entry (L3PTE) associated with each page of virtual address space contains an owner field (see Figure 2.12) that specifies which access mode owns the page. The memory management system service checks the owner field to determine whether the service's requestor has an access mode at least as privileged as the owner mode of the page and thus is able to manipulate the page in the desired fashion.

In general, a process is only permitted to affect P0, P1, and P2 address space, not system space, with these services. The only exception is when a process uses the buffer object services to double-map process-private address space into system space.

Almost all the memory management system services accept a desired virtual address range as one or more input arguments. Many of the services can partly succeed, that is, affect only a portion of the specified address range. A system service indicates partial success by returning an error status and the address range for which the operation completed.

Common Characteristics of the 32-Bit System Services

Many of the 32-bit memory management system services have similar structures and sequences and similar arguments. The input range for a 32-bit service is specified by the address of a two-longword array, the INADR argument. The first longword is the starting address, and the second, the address of the last byte to be created. The RETADR argument is the address of a two-longword array that receives the addresses of the starting and ending bytes actually created. The ACMODE argument specifies the owner of the address space, the least privileged mode that can access it.

Each 32-bit system service first executes code generated by a MACRO-32 macro that tests whether enough arguments have been supplied and, if not, returns the error status SS$_INSFARG to the requestor.

Each service validates its arguments. A typical service makes the following checks:

- It tests the accessibility of the INADR and RETADR arguments.

- It maximizes the ACMODE argument with the mode of the service requestor.

- It tests the starting and ending addresses and, if either is a system space address, returns the error status SS$_NOPRIV.

The service then explicitly creates scratch space on the stack to record information about the service request.

The macro $MMGDEF defines symbolic offsets into this scratch space, which is pointed to by the frame pointer (FP) register while the system service procedure is executing. Figure D-1 shows the layout of the scratch space on the stack. Some fields are used by only a few system services; others are common to all.

MMG$L_MMG_FLAGS contains flag bits associated with the operation. Some of the 64-bit services use these same flags, passing them to inner mode routines as an argument.

- Bit MMG$V_CHGPAGFIL in this longword, when set, means page file quota should be charged for the operation.

```
┌─────────────────────────────┐
│          PGFLCNT            │
├─────────────────────────────┤
│       PAGCNT / EFBLK        │
├─────────────────────────────┤
│          VFYFLAGS           │
├─────────────────────────────┤
│          SVSTARTVA          │
├─────────────────────────────┤
│          PAGESUBR           │
├─────────────────────────────┤
│          SAVRETADR          │
├─────────────────────────────┤
│          CALLEDIPL          │
├─────────────────────────────┤
│          PER_PAGE           │
├─────────────────────────────┤
│         ACCESS_MODE         │
├─────────────────────────────┤
│          MMG_FLAGS          │
FP ├─────────────────────────────┤
```

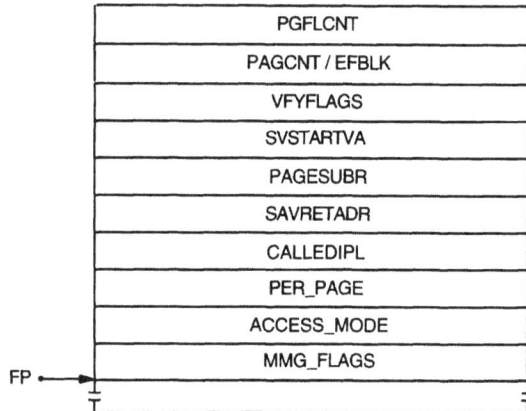

Figure D-1 Layout of Scratch Space on the Stack

- Bit MMG$V_NOWAIT_IPL0, when set, means that a memory management
  routine should return with an error status rather than waiting at interrupt
  priority level (IPL) 0 for I/O completion.

- Bit MMG$V_NO_OVERMAP, when set, means that address space to be created
  may not overlap existing address space.

- Bit MMG$V_PARTIAL_FIRST, when set, means that the first page to be
  mapped is only partially backed by section file.

- Bit MMG$V_PARTIAL_LAST, when set, means that the last page to be mapped
  is only partially backed by section file.

- Bit MMG$V_NO_IRP_DELETE, when set, means that an I/O request packet
  created by the $UPDSEC system service is currently in use and should not be
  deallocated to nonpaged pool.

- Bit MMG$V_DELPAG_NOP, when set, means that not all pages in the specified
  region could be deleted.

- Bit MMG$V_CLUSTER_DEL, when set, means that the per-page deletion
  routine can delete a whole cluster of pages at once.

- Bit MMG$V_WINDOW, when set, means that the page is part of a
  memoryresident global section or a section mapped by page frame number
  (PFN).

- Bit MMG$V_SHARED_L3PTS, when set, means that the page is part of a memoryresident global section that is mapped with shared page tables.

- Bit MMG$V_RWAST_AT_IPL0, when set, means that the per-page deletion routine (see Section 3.10.2) should wait the kernel thread at IPL 0 rather than IPL 2. The bit is set by the $DELTVA and $DELTVA_64 system services. The IPL 0 wait enables Extended QIO Processor (XQP) kernel mode asynchronous system traps (ASTs) to be delivered, preventing a deadlock in certain circumstances. MMG$L_ACCESS_MODE contains the access mode associated with the operation, the maximized ACMODE argument.

MMG$L_PER_PAGE is the per-page processing context area. It contains one defined flag, MMG$V_DELGBLDON. When set, the bit means that global pages in the range have already been deleted.

MMG$L_CALLEDIPL records the IPL from which the service was requested, typically 0.

MMG$L_SAVRETADR contains the value of the optional service RETADR argument.

MMG$L_PAGESUBR contains the procedure value of the executive routine that performs the requested service on a single page.

MMG$L_SVSTARTVA saves the starting virtual address specified by the service requestor.

MMG$L_VFYFLAGS contains the section flags passed as an argument to a service such as $CRMPSC and verified by the service.

MMG$L_PAGCNT and MMG$L_EFBLK are two names for the same field. MMG$L_PAGCNT, used by services related to buffer objects, contains the number of pages in a buffer object being created or deleted. MMG$L_EFBLK contains the number of the end-of-file block for a section file.

MMG$L_PGFLCNT contains the number of pages of page file quota that have been reserved against the job's quota for this request.

After creating and initializing the scratch space on the stack, a 32-bit memory management system service takes the following steps:

1. It performs argument validation.

2. It raises IPL to 2 to block the delivery of an AST. In addition to blocking process deletion, this prevents the execution of AST code that could cause unexpected changes to the page tables, working set list, region descriptor entries (RDEs), and other data structures.

3. If appropriate, it checks page ownership to ensure that a less privileged access mode is not attempting to alter the properties of pages owned by a more privileged access mode.

4. It calls the routine MMG$CREDEL, in module SYSCREDEL, passing it the procedure value of a per-page service-specific routine to accomplish the desired action of the system service. MMG$CREDEL performs general page processing and calls the per-page routine for each page in the desired range.

5. It reprobes write accessibility of any output arguments.

6. It returns the address range actually affected by MMG$CREDEL's actions in the optional RETADR argument.

7. It restores the entry IPL and returns to its requestor.

In some cases, step 4 in that sequence is replaced by calling a routine that affects all pages in the desired range.

MMG$CREDEL takes the following steps:

1. It tests the starting and ending addresses of the range and, if either is in system space, returns the error status SS$_NOPRIV.

2. It initializes MMG$L_PAGESUBR and MMG$L_SVSTARTVA in the scratch space and loads registers with information such as process control block (PCB) address, process header (PHD) address, page count, starting virtual address, and ending virtual address.

3. MMG$CREDEL calls the per-page routine. Unless the routine returns an error status, MMG$CREDEL continues to call it, once per page.

4. If the per-page routine returns the status SS$_REGISFULL, MMG$CREDEL converts it to SS$_VASFULL.

5. When an error occurs or there are no more pages, MMG$CREDEL returns to its caller with a status code and the address of the last affected page.

Common Characteristics of the 64-Bit System Services

The 64-bit system services have a common structure and sequence and similar arguments. They do not explicitly use scratch space on the stack.

A 64-bit service typically takes the following steps:

1. It performs argument validation, for example:

    — These services are written in C and must explicitly test whether too few or too many arguments have been supplied. Each checks the number of arguments and, if incorrect, returns either the error status SS$_INSFARG or SS$_TOO_MANY_ARGS.

    — It checks that output arguments are accessible and, if not, returns the error status SS$_ACCVIO.

    — If the service has a FLAGS argument, it checks that only valid flags were set in the argument and, if not, returns the error status SS$_IVSECFLG.

    — It maximizes the ACMODE argument.

2. It raises IPL to 2 to block AST delivery.

3. If appropriate, it checks page ownership.

4. It loops, calling a per-page service-specific routine, typically the same routine as its 32-bit counterpart.

5. It reprobes write accessibility of any output arguments.

6. It returns the address range actually affected in the RETURN_VA_64 and RETURN_LENGTH_64 arguments.

7. It restores the entry IPL and returns to its requestor.

Virtual Address Region Creation

The Create Virtual Region ($CREATE_REGION_64) system service is requested to create a region within process-private address space.

Service arguments include the desired length, protection, and flags that specify whether the region is in P0, P1, or P2 space; whether its allocation is to be ascending or descending; whether address space within it should be created automatically in response to an access violation; whether it should be permanent; and whether its space is capable of being mapped with shared page tables. Only memory-resident global sections and Galaxywide global sections are mapped into such a region.

The service creates a region with the requested characteristics, assigns an ID to it, and returns its ID and address.

The $CREATE_REGION_64 system service procedure, EXE$CREATE_REGION_64 in module SYS_REGIONS, runs in kernel mode. EXE$CREATE_REGION_64 takes the following steps:

1. It calculates the number of PTEs in a page table page and the number of bytes mapped by an L3PT.

2. In addition to making the checks described in Section 3.1.2, it validates its arguments as follows:

    a. It checks that REGION_PROT is valid, returning SS$_IVPROTECT if not.

    b. It maximizes the create and owner access mode fields in the REGION_PROT argument with that of the requestor. It checks that the owner mode is less or equally privileged to the creator mode, returning SS$_IVREGPROT if not.

    c. It checks that the LENGTH_64 argument is nonzero and a multiple of the size of a page, returning the error status SS$_LEN_NOTPAGMULT if not.

    d. If VA$V_SHARED_PTS in the FLAGS argument is clear, EXE$CREATE_REGION_64 checks that the optional START_VA_64 argument, if supplied, is on a page-aligned boundary and returns the error status SS$_VA_NOTPAGALGN if not.

    e. e. If VA$V_SHARED_PTS in the FLAGS argument is set, indicating that the region can be mapped by shared page tables, EXE$CREATE_REGION_64 checks that the START_VA_64 argument is a multiple of the number of bytes mapped by one L3PT. On a system with an 8 KB page size, an L3PT maps 8 MB. It also rounds up the LENGTH_64 argument to such a multiple.

    f. f. It calculates the address of the process-permanent RDE corresponding to the specified address space.

    g. It checks that the LENGTH_64 argument can be expressed in the number of significant address bits for the system's page size and page table hierarchy, for example, 43 bits for a page size of 8 KB and a three-level page table. If not, it returns the error status SS$_VASFULL.

  h. h. If the START_VA_64 argument was supplied, it checks that the sum of the START_VA_64 and LENGTH_64 arguments can be expressed in that number of bits, returning SS$_VASFULL if not. It also checks that the START_VA_64 and the sum of START_VA_64 and LENGTH_64 are within the process-permanent region specified in the FLAGS argument, returning SS$_VA_IN_USE if not.

3. It raises IPL to 2.

4. It allocates an RDE from the P1 allocation region and initializes it with information from the service arguments. It initializes RDE$Q_REGION_ID from the contents of PHD$Q_NEXT_REGION_ID and increments them.

5. If the argument START_VA_64 was not specified, it determines the alignment requirement for the starting address.

  — For a region without shared page tables, the starting address merely needs to be page-aligned.

  — For a region with shared page tables, EXE$CREATE_REGION_64 first attempts a 512-page alignment so that the shared pages can potentially be mapped as a 512-page granularity hint region. It scans the list of user-defined RDEs within the specified process-permanent region, looking for an unused piece of address space with at least the specified alignment and size. If it fails to find one and this is a shared page table region, it tries again, shrinking the desired alignment to the next smaller granularity hint region size, 64 pages, and then, if necessary, to eight pages, and finally to one page. If it fails to find an unused piece with single-page alignment that is large enough, it deallocates the RDE and returns SS$_VA_IN_USE to its requestor.

6. If START_VA_64 was specified, it scans the list of user-defined RDEs within the specified process-permanent region, which are ordered by virtual address. It looks for the place at which the new RDE should be inserted.

  — If the address range of the new RDE overlaps the range of an existing userdefined RDE, EXE$CREATE_REGION_64 deallocates the new RDE and returns the error status SS$_VA_IN_USE to its requestor.

— If there is overlap with the process-permanent region, it adjusts that region so that it ends where the new one begins.

7. It inserts the RDE into the list and also at the front of the region ID list.

8. It lowers IPL.

9. It records peak page file use and virtual size statistics, and stores return information about the newly created RDE in the RETURN_VA_64, RETURN_REGION_ID_64, and RETURN_LENGTH_64 arguments. It returns SS$_NORMAL to its requestor.

The material in Appendix D is drawn from Chapter 3 of Ruth E. Goldenberg, *OpenVMS Alpha Internals and Data Structures: Memory Management*, 1-55558-159-5, Digital Press, 2002, © Compaq Information Technologies Group, L.P.

Appendix E — Symbols, Data, and Expressions

By Paul C. Anagnostopoulos and Steve Hoffman

This appendix begins an examination of DCL facilities that make it useful as a general-purpose programming language. The focus of this appendix is on data and the manipulation of data.

Symbols

A symbol is the DCL equivalent of what most programming languages call a variable. A symbol is a named entity with which you can associate an item of data. Later on, the data can be retrieved and manipulated by using the name to refer to it. The item of data is called the symbol's value. The same symbol may have different values at different points in the program. It is the ability of a symbol to take on different values that makes it such a powerful programming tool. A DCL symbol has three items of information associated with it:

- *Name* Each symbol has a name that is used to refer to it. The name of a symbol, together with its level, uniquely distinguishes if from all other existing symbols.

- *Level* Each symbol has a level, which is determined by the context in which the symbol was originally created. The various symbol contexts are described in Section 3.3. A symbol with the same name may exist in two different contexts, but duplicate names may not exist in the same context.

Therefore, a symbol's name and level uniquely distinguish it from all other symbols.

- *Value* Each symbol has a value associated with it. The value is an item of data that can be manipulated by referring to it by way of the symbol's name. In other words, the symbol name acts as a "handle" for the data item.

A symbol name is composed of letters, digits, dollar sign ($), and underscore (_), but its first character cannot be a digit. Use of the dollar sign is reserved to DIGITAL. Youmay type a symbol name in lowercase or uppercase letters; DCL converts the name to uppercase before doing anything with it. A symbol name is limited to 255 characters in length. The symbol value is an item of data, associatedwith the symbol, that can be accessed using the symbol name. In DCL, data items can be integers or character strings.

Here is a simple example to illustrate the creation of a symbol:

```
$ sym1 = 42
```

This is an assignment command, which creates a new symbol. The symbol has the four-character name SYM1, a level determined by the context of the assignment command, and the value 42, which is an integer. Once a symbol is created, its value can be replaced with a new value by performing another assignment command:

```
$ sym1 = "I'd rather be sailing"
```

This command does not create a new symbol but rather replaces the existing symbol's value with the character string "I'd rather be sailing". An assignment command creates the symbol if it does not already exist and then sets it to the value specified on the right-hand side of the command.

It is difficult to fully appreciate the power of symbols without some further background. The rest of this chapter describes symbols, data items, and assignment commands in detail.

Types of Data

The ultimate purpose of every program is to create and manipulate data. The collective term data refers to all the information available to, or generated by, a program. This data is composed of individual data items, each of which can be manipulated separately from the rest. In DCL, a data item has an associated data type, which signifies what kind of data it is. Strictly speaking, DCL supports two types of data: integers and character strings. However, a 24 Symbols, Data, and Expressions particularly useful third type of data, Boolean data, can be implemented with the first two. The following sections discuss these data types.

Every data item has two representations, an internal one and an external one. The internal representation is determined by the host computer, which for DCL is the OpenVMS VAX or Alpha system. Almost all computers operate in binary, representing data items as numbers in base 2. Each binary digit is called a bit, so we speak in terms of data occupying a certain number of bits of computer memory.

Computer users aremuch happierwhen data can be represented in natural forms such as decimal numbers or letters of the alphabet. These familiar forms are the external representations of the data, and all programming languages provide for them.When the external representation of a data item appears in a program, it is called a literal. The following DCL command contains two literals:

```
$ write sys$output "The answer is ", 13
```

The first literal is the character string "The answer is" and the second is the decimal integer 13.

Integers

An integer is a whole number, which can be negative, zero, or positive. DCL supports signed integers that occupy 32 bits of memory, thus restricting them to the range from -2,147,483,648 to +2,147,483,647. In the VAX and Alpha architectures, a 32-bit quantity is referred to as a longword. Although the internal representation of an integer is in binary, the external representation is made up of digits and other characters, which allows a "natural" specification of the number.

Integer literals can be represented in base 10 (decimal), base 16 (hexadecimal), or base 8 (octal). Decimal integers are discussed in this section, and hexadecimal integers inAppendix A. Octal integers are rarely used andwill not be discussed in this book. A decimal integer is composed of the ten decimal digits 0–9, optionally preceded by a plus sign (+) or minus (-). Punctuation marks such as commas are not allowed in integers. The following are examples of decimal integers:

```
0  7  07  42  +3286  1  -39840938
```

Character Strings

A character string is a sequence of individual characters. A character can be an actual glyph, such as an uppercase A or a plus sign (+). Glyphs are usually called printable characters. A character can also be a control character, which does not represent a glyph but rather a formatting operation, such as tab or line feed. Each distinct character is assigned a code number, and the complete collection of characters and their code numbers is called a character set. The VAX and Alpha architectures employ the ASCII character set (ASCII stands for American Standard Code for Information Interchange) subset of the ISO Latin 1 character set. In both ISO Latin 1 and in ASCII, the characters occupy eight bits and the code numbers range from 0 to 255.

The number of individual characters in a character string is called its length. A character string can be composed of any number of characters from 1 to approximately 900. The upper limit depends on the context in which the string is used. A character string can also contain no characters at all, in which case it is called the null string.

A character string literal is represented by enclosing its constituent characters in a set of double quotes ("). Here are a few examples:

```
""  "x"  "X"  "*"  "a short string"
"This is a sentence complete with punctuation."
```

The first example is the null string. You can represent any printable character in a string literal, but there is no way to represent control characters. A special case is made of the double quote character: you must represent each double quote character in the literal with an adjacent pair of double quotes:

```
"This string contains ""a quoted phrase""."
```

The string literal shown here consists of six words, the last three of which are inside double quotes. Each double quote that is part of the literal, but not the ones that enclose the literal, must be paired. It is a common mistake to forget to pair the double quotes inside a string:

```
"This string contains "a quoted phrase"."
```

It appears toDCL that the string literal ends with the space following the word contains and that the final three words are not part of the string literal.

Booleans

The Boolean data type encompasses the two logic values true and false. Logical values are important in programming because true/false, yes/no decisions are constantly being made by a program in order to guide its flow of execution. Many conventional programming languages distinguish the Boolean data type from other data types, but DCL does not. However, the Boolean data type can be simulated using the integer and character string data types.WheneverDCL needs a true/false value to use with a logical operation, it accepts an integer or character string and interprets it as true or false depending on its value.

Table E-1 specifies how this interpretation is made.

Table E-1: DCL's interpretation of data as Boolean values

Boolean value	Data so interpreted
TRUE	Odd integers; character strings beginning with t, T, y or Y; character strings representing odd integers (e.g.,"381")
FALSE	Even integers; all other character strings

The following data items are considered true:

```
1 3 "True" "Y" "Yes" "yupsters"
```

The following are considered false:

```
0 2 "False" "N" "No" "nope"
"random!nonsense" "380"
```

Symbolic literals for the two Boolean values true and false round out the simulation of the Boolean data type. DCL provides no such literals, so the authors choose the symbols TRUE and FALSE to represent them. Thses symbols can be established with the assignment command described in the next section.

Assignment Commands

The assignment command is the means by which DCL symbols are created and assigned values. Because most languages refer to their commands as statements, the assignment command is often called assignment statement. The assignment statement has the following general format:

```
$ symbol = expression
```

The symbol named on the left-hand side of the equal sign is assigned the value determined by the expression on the right-hand side. For example:

```
$ my_name = "Brian Cutler"
```

Here the symbol MY_NAME is assigned the character string "Brian Cutler". We read the assignment statement as "MY_NAME gets "Brian Cutler"" and say that the symbol MY_NAME is set to the value of the expression "Brian Cutler". The word equals is not used when discussing the action of an assignment statement because it is too easily confusedwith the idea of equality for comparison purposes, as in "1 does not equal 2." Integer and string literals are examples of simple expressions; a literal can appear by itself on the righthand side of an assignment statement. Section 3.4 describes expressions in detail.

A symbol is created the first time a command is used to assign it a value. Subsequent assignments to the same symbol discard the current value and replace it with the new value. A symbol can have an integer value at one point in the program and a character string value at another point. The data type is associated with the value, not with the symbol, as it is in many languages such as Pascal. Because the data type is associated with the value and not with the symbol, a symbol can be set to any type of data. The following assignment statements illustrate these rules:

```
$ days_per_year = 366
$ days_per_leap_year = days_per_year
$ days_per_year = 365
$ days_per_leap_year = "three hundred sixty-six"
```

In the second assignment statement, the symbol DAYS_PER_LEAP_YEAR is set to the value of the previously created symbol DAYS_PER_YEAR. A symbol by itself is another example of a simple expression on the right-hand side of an assignment command. Note that DAYS_PER_LEAP_YEAR is assigned both types of data at different times. In addition to its name and value, each symbol has a level. The name and the level together uniquely identify the symbol from among all existing symbols. A symbol's level is determined by the context in which it is created and by the kind of assignment statement used to create it. The following sections describe the different levels: prompt level, procedure level, and global level.

DCL Prompt Level

Symbols created at theDCL prompt are associatedwith theDCL prompt level. You might create such a symbol to remember something to do later:

```
$ note = "Remember to call Jim before leaving."
```

This symbol is at the prompt level because it was created with an assignment statement at the DCL prompt. You can display the value of the symbol with the SHOW SYMBOL command (you type the first line, and OpenVMS responds with the second line):

```
$ show symbol note
NOTE = "Remember to call Jim before leaving."
```

The symbol can be used to create another symbol at the prompt level:

```
$ old_note = note
$ note = "Don't forget to pick up the video tape"
```

Now two prompt-level symbols exist, NOTE and OLD_NOTE. Symbols at the prompt level remain in existence during your entire login period unless explicitly deleted.

Procedure Level

Each DCL command procedure has its own symbol level. When you invoke a procedure with the at-sign (@) command, a new level is established. Any symbols created by the procedure are associated with the procedure's level. If the procedure invokes another procedure, the second procedure has its own level and its symbols are associated with its level. In this way, each procedure has a set of symbols that "belong" to it.

Here is a simple procedure named SIMPLE-PROC:

```
$ name = "OpenVMS is VMS"
$ show symbol name
```

When invoked, this procedure creates the procedure-level symbol NAME and assigns a character string to it. The procedure then displays the value of the symbol:

```
$ @simple-proc
NAME = "OpenVMS is VMS"
```

When a procedure terminates, all the symbols created at its level are deleted. Since the symbols are associated with the procedure's level, it makes no sense for them to exist once the procedure has terminated. Should the procedure be invoked again, its symbols will be recreated from scratch by DCL; they will have lost their old values.

A procedure can refer to a symbol at the prompt level as long as the symbol does not have the same name as a symbol created by the procedure. If symbols with the same name are created at the prompt and procedure levels, the one at procedure level "shadows" or "hides" the one at prompt level. Similarly, a subprocedure invoked from a main procedure can refer to symbols created by the main procedure. For example, if procedure A invokes procedure B, B can refer to the symbols created by A. The ability to use symbols created at an outer level allows you to write a procedure that displays the NOTE symbol created at the prompt level:

```
$! Procedure to display the note.
$
$ write sys$output "Your note is:"
$ show symbol note
```

The WRITE command displays the text in double quotes. The SHOW SYMBOL command refers to the NOTE symbol created at the prompt level. Because this little procedure does not create its own symbol named NOTE, the reference to NOTE gets the symbol at prompt level. The display produced by this procedure is shown here:

```
Your note is:
Note = "Don't forget to pick up the video tape."
```

When DCL is executing a procedure and needs the value of a symbol, it performs a simple search process. As soon as it finds a symbol with the given name, it terminates the search and uses the value of the symbol. Here is the process as described so far:

1. DCL looks for the symbol among the symbols created by the currently executing procedure.

2. If the procedure was invoked by another procedure, DCL looks for the symbol among the invoking procedure's symbols.

3. Step 2 is repeated for each additional level of command procedure

4. DCL looks for the symbol among the symbols created at DCL prompt level.

Although a procedure can use the values of symbols at outer levels, it cannot create or change symbols at outer levels. This is somewhat restrictive, so a special global level exists to solve the problem.

Global Level

Sophisticated DCL applications are composed of multiple procedures, which invoke one another in various combinations. Sometimes it is necessary for a procedure B to calculate a value and pass it back to another procedureA, which invoked it.With what you know so far, there is no way to accomplish this. If B stores the value in a symbol at its own level, that symbol will be deleted when B terminates. The alternative is for B to store the value in a symbol at A's level, butDCL provides no means of doing so. The global symbol level exists to solve this dilemma.

Symbols created at the global level are called global symbols. You must explicitly request that a global symbol be created by using a variant of the assignment statement:

```
$ xda_answer == 42
```

Note that two equal signs are used in the example. The double equal sign requests that the symbol XDA_ANSWER be created at the global level and assigned the value 42. Global symbols are only created when you use the double equal sign form of the assignment command.

By convention, global symbol names begin with the application facility code and a single underscore. In the preceding example, the facility code is XDA.

Global symbols can always be created, whether you are at theDCL prompt or executing a command procedure. This capability is what distinguishes global symbols from prompt-level symbols and is the only major difference between the two kinds of symbols. The double equal sign forces a global symbol to be created regardless of the level at which the assignment statement is executed. Subsequent global assignment to the same symbol changes the global symbol's value. The value of a global symbol can be obtained at any level as long as there are no symbols of the same name at a procedure level or prompt level. To accommodate global symbols, the symbol search process is extended to its final form:

1. DCL looks for the symbol among the symbols created by the currently executing procedure.

2. If the procedure was invoked by another procedure, DCL looks for the symbol among the invoking procedure's symbols.

3. Step 2 is repeated for each additional level of command procedure.

---

4. DCL looks for the symbol among the symbols created at prompt level.

5. DCL looks for the symbol among the global symbols. The following simple example illustrates a subprocedure that creates a global symbol in order to pass a value back to its calling procedure:

```
$! This is procedure A
$
$ @b ! B will set global symbol XDA_ANSWER
$! This is procedure B
$
$ xda_answer == 42
$ exit
```

Procedure A invokes procedure B to establish the global value. Procedure B creates the global symbol XDA_ANSWER using a double equal sign assignment statement. It then exits, allowing procedureAto continue. ProcedureAdisplays the value of the global symbol. Because XDA_ANSWER is global, it is not deleted when procedure B exits, thus allowing A to obtain its value. It is quite easy to omit the second equal sign when you mean to perform a global assignment. Look at the following code:

```
$ xda_answer == 42
.
.
.
$ xda_answer = 43 ! Meant to use ==
$ show symbol xda_answer
```

The first assignment command creates the global symbol XDA_ANSWER and assigns it the value 42. The second assignment command was intended to change the value of the global symbol, but only one equal sign is present. Therefore, the assignment command creates a procedure-level symbol with the same name, XDA_ANSWER. This procedure-level symbol hides the global symbol. The SHOW command displays 43 quite nicely, but the global symbol still has the value 42. Be careful always to use two equal signs when performing global assignments.

Global symbols remain in existence during your entire login period, unless explicitly deleted.

Symbol Scope

Symbol scoping allows a cautiously written, modular command procedure to avoid unintended and undesirable interactions involving symbols. Scoping does not delete any existing symbols; it controls the visibility of symbols in the current procedure level.

You can control symbol scoping using the SET SCOPE command. When SET SCOPE is called at a procedure level, it can hide the global symbols, the local symbols created at any outer procedure levels, or both, from the current procedure scope. SET SCOPE can also be used avoid problems where one or more symbols might conflict with DCL command verbs.

When the procedure level that called SET SCOPE exits, the scoping rules for the outer level are restored.

Expressions

An assignment statement assigns a value to a symbol. The value is determined by an expression on the right-hand side of the equal sign. Expressions are also used in otherDCL commands, such as the IF command. Literals and symbols have already been used as simple expressions. When used in an expression, a literal stands for itself and a symbol stands for its current value. These simple expressions are useful but not powerful enough to compute new values, such as the sum of two integers.

New values are computed using expressions composed of operators and operands. An operator is a character or sequence of characters that stands for some mathematical operation, such as multiplication, or for a string operation, such as concatenation. The operands associated with an operator determine the values that are to participate in the operation. Here is a simple expression:

```
a * b
```

This denotes that the value of the symbol A is to be multiplied by the value of the symbol B to produce a new value. The gate of the new value is determined by the context in which the expression appears. So far, the only context in which an expression can appear is the assignment statement:

```
$ product = a * b
```

Here, the product of the values of A and B is assigned to the symbol PRODUCT. WhenDCL encounters an expression, it applies the operators to their operands in a certain predetermined order, producing a final result that is assigned to a symbol or used for some other purpose. When DCL processes an expression in this manner, we say that DCL evaluates the expression.

In order to completely understand expressions, youmust become familiar with the available operators, the operands they expect, and the order in which the operators are applied to their operands. Tables E-2, E-3, and E-4 describe the operators provided by DCL for use with integer, character string and Boolean values, respectively. Table E-5 illustrates the order in which operators are applied.

Not all operators require two operands as multiplication does. Some require only one operand. (In the C language there is an operator that requires three operands.) The number of operands required by an operator is called its arity.

Operators with arity of 2 are called binary operators. Those with an arity of 1 are called unary operators. A few examples:

Table E-2: Integer operators

Operator	Arity	Result type	Result value
+	Unary	Integer	Integer operand unchanged.
-	Unary	Integer	Negative of integer operand.
+	Binary	Integer	Sum of integer operands.
-	Binary	Integer	Difference of integer operands.
*	Binary	Integer	Product of integer operands.
/	Binary	Integer	Quotient of integer operands, truncated toward zero.
.EQ.	Binary	Boolean	True if integer operands are equal, false otherwise.
.NE.	Binary	Boolean	True if integer operands are unequal, false otherwise.
.GT.	Binary	Boolean	True if first integer operand is greater than second, false otherwise.
.GE.	Binary	Boolean	True if first integer operand is greater than or equal to second, false otherwise.
.LT.	Binary	Boolean	True if first integer operand is less than second, false otherwise.
.LE.	Binary	Boolean	True if first integer operand is less than or equal to second, false otherwise.
.NOT.	Unary	Integer	Bitwise Boolean NOT of integer operand. A bit in the result is 1 if the corresponding bit in the operand is zero, and vice versa.

Operator	Arity	Result type	Result value
.AND.	Binary	Integer	Bitwise Boolean AND of integer operands. A bit in the result is 1 if both of the corresponding bits in the operands are 1.
.OR.	Binary	Integer	Bitwise Boolean inclusive OR of integer operands. A bit in the result of 1 if either or both of the corresponding bits in the operands are 1.

```
$ sum = a + b - c
$ sum = -sum
$ positive = sum .gt. 0
$ negative = not. Positive
```

The first example contains an expression composed of two binary operators. The operands for the plus operator are A and B; the operands for the minus operator are the resulting sum and C. The second example uses the unary minus operator to negate its operand. Notice how the hyphen character is used as two different operators with different arities, its meaning determined by context. The third example uses the binary "greater than" operator to compare two numbers. The final example uses the unary "not" operator to invert its Boolean operand. The operator tables specify the arity and meaning of every DCL operator.

Table E-3: Character string operators

Operator	Arity	Result type	Result value
*	Binary	String	A copy of the first string operand with a copy of the second one concatenated to it (e.g., "Hello-" + "there." produces "Hello-there.").
-	Binary	String	A copy of the first string operand with the leftmost occurence of the second one removed from it (e.g., "oh-why-oh-why" - "why" produces "oh--oh-why").

Table E-3: Character string operators (Continued)

Operator	Arity	Result type	Result value
.EQS.	Binary	Boolean	True if string operands contain the same character sequence, false otherwise.
.NES.	Binary	Boolean	True if string operands contain different character sequences, false otherwise.
.GTS.	Binary	Boolean	True if first string operand is alphabetically greater than second, false otherwise. The collating sequence is based on the ASCII character set.
.GES.	Binary	Boolean	True if first string operand is greater than or equal to second, false otherwise.
.LTS.	Binary	Boolean	True if first string operand is less than second, false otherswise.
.LES.	Binary	Boolean	True if first string operand is less than or equal to second, false otherwise.

Table E-4: Boolean operators

Operator	Arity	Result type	Result value
.NOT.	Unary	Boolean	True if Boolean operands is false, false if it is true.
.AND.	Binary	Boolean	True if both Boolean operands are true, false otherwise. There is no guarantee about which operand is evaluated first.
.OR.	Binary	Boolean	True if either or both Boolean operands are true, false otherwise. There is no guarantee about which operand is evaluated first.

Table E-5: Operator precedence

Precedence	Operator
8 (highest)	( )
7	unary + -
6	* /
5	binary + -
4	.EQ. .NE. .GT. .GE. .LT. .LT. .EQS. .NES. .GTS. .GES. .LTS.
3	.NOT.
2	.AND.
1	(lowest) .OR.

The order in which operators are applied to operands is determined by operator precedence. Table E-5 lists the precedence of the DCL operators. An operator with a high precedence is applied before an operator with a lower precedence, regardless of the order of their appearance in the expression. Every operator is assigned a precedence so that the order of application can be determined without ambiguity. Here are a few expressions to illustrate operator precedence:

```
$ value = a * b + c
$ value = c + a * b
$ value = a * b - c * d
$ value = -x + y
```

Because multiplication has a higher precedence than addition, the first two examples both multiply by A by B before adding C. This is true even though, in the second example, the multiply operator appears after the add operator. The order of evaluation is determined by operator precedence, not merely by order of appearance. The third example calculates the product of A and B, and then the product of C and D, and finally subtracts one product from the other. The fourth example negates X and then adds Y; the precedence of unary minus is higher than that of addition. If there are two or more operators of equal precedence in an expression, such as the multiply operators in the third example above, the operators are evaluated from left to right. In the third example, A * B is evaluated before C * D.

Sometimes the order of evaluation determined by operator precedence is not what you want. Parentheses are used to force operators to be evaluated in a certain order regardless of their precedence.When parentheses surround a portion of an expression, that portion is evaluated before the surrounding expression, regardless of precedence. Here are the preceding examples with parentheses added:

```
$ value = a * (b + c)
$ value = (c + a) * b
$ value = a * (b - c) * d
$ value = -(x + y)
```

The first example now calculates the sum of B and C and then multiplies it by A. The sum appears in parentheses, so it is evaluated first, even though the precedence ofmultiplication is higher. The second one adds C and A and then multiplies the sum of B. The third example subtracts C from B, multiplies the difference by A, and then multiplies that result by D. The final example adds X and Y and negates the resulting sum. In each case, the final value is different when parentheses are used.

As DCL evaluates an expression, it must decide whether each operand represents an integer, string, or Boolean value. In some cases, the type of the operands actually affects the meaning of the operator. Such a case is the plus (+) operator, which performs addition when its operands are integers, but performs string concatenation when its operands are character strings. DCL uses the following rules to match operators and operand types:

- If the operator accepts only integer operands (e.g., * for multiply), then any string operands are first converted to integers.

- If the operator accepts only string operands (e.g., .EQS. for string compare equal), then any integer operands are first converted to strings.

- If the operator accepts either integers or strings (e.g., + for add or concatenate) and its operands are of different types, then integers win over strings and the string operand is first converted to an integer. For example, if you attempt to add an integer and a string, the string is first converted to an integer.

- If the operator is a Boolean operator (e.g., .AND. for logical and), then the operands are interpreted as Boolean values according to the rules given in Table E-1.

Astring can be converted to an integer as long as it contains a valid external representation of an integer (e.g., "-372" can be converted to -372). If it does not, it is converted to the integer 0. An integer can always be converted to a string by simply creating a string containing its external representation. Because these operator/operand matching rules are complicated, it is best to avoid using operators with mixed operand types. You can explicitly request that a string be converted to an integer, or vice versa, using the lexical functions F$INTEGER and F$STRING presented in the next section.

The material in Appendix E is drawn from Chapter 3 of Paul C. Anagnostopoulos and Steve Hoffman, *Writing Real Programs in DCL, 2nd Edition*, 1-55558-191-9, Digital Press, 1999, © Butterworth-Heinemann.

Index

TCP/IP, 101–4

O

ODS-2, 10–11
ODS-5, 10, 12
OpenVMS
    Cluster, 109
    command, 6–10
    document reference, 6
    error messages, 9
    failure, 29
    files and devices, 10–15
    history, 1
    installations, 1
    on Itanium, 5
    license management facility (LMF), 37
    logical definitions, 15–16
    ODS-2, 10–11
    ODS-5, 10, 12
    platform, 4–5
    profile, 44
    RAID support, 12, 113, 114
    rooted file tree support, 12
    superusers, 20
    support, 1–2
    symbols, 16–17
    tutorial, 6–20
OpenVMS Concurrent-Use License, 33–34
    contents, 33–34
    defined, 33
    See also Licenses
OpenVMS Management Station, 55, 65–66
    management tasks, 65
    uses, 66
Operating System Base License, 33

P

PALcode, 6
Passwords, 20, 90–91
    history, 90
    number of, 90
    resetting, 46
    unacceptable, 90
    See also Security

Performance management, 81–82
    baseline measurements, 82
    issues, resolving, 82
    programs, 83
    requirements, 81
Performance monitoring, 81–87
    AUTOGEN, 83–85, 87
    introduction to, 81–83
    real-time, 85–87
    resources, 82
Physical memory quota, 19–20
PostScript printing, 59–60, 66
Preemptive scheduling, 19
PRINT command, 63, 65
Printer control libraries, 63–65, 66
    contents, examining, 64
    creating, 64–65
    default, 64
    files, 65
    modifying, 64
    need for, 63
Printer forms, 62–63, 66
    characteristics definition, 62
    defined, 62
    multiple, 62
    queue association, 62
    requesting, 63
Printers
    farms, 61–62, 66
    LAT, 58, 59
    setup with DCPS, 59
    TCP/IP, 60–61
Print queues, 57–59, 66
    default protection on, 94
    entries, deleting, 61
    generic, 61
    multiple, 61
    PostScript, 59–60, 66
    printer forms association, 62
    viewing, 61
Privileged images, 20
Privileges
    ALTPRI (Alter Priority), 95
    assigning, 95
    BYPASS, 96

controlling, 95–96
EXQUOTA (Exceed Quota), 95
SETPRV (Set Privilege), 96
VOLPRO (Volume Protection), 96
Processes, 17–20
creation, 18
physical memory quota, 19–20
priority, 19
quota limits, 18
size limit definition, 19
STARTUP, 24, 25
SWAPPER, 24
Product authorization kit (PAK), 36–37, 41
information management, 37–38
loading, 39
registering, 39
for volume shadowing, 37
PRODUCT command, 39

Q

Queue manager, 55–56, 66
load leveling, 57, 61
print and batch, 55–56
starting, 55
Queues, 55–66
batch, 56–57, 66
DCPS, 60
generic, 61
management of, 55
print, 57–59, 66
support, 55
TCP/IP, 60–61
Quota limits, 18–19

R

RAID support, 12, 113, 114
Real-time performance monitoring, 85–87
RECALL command, 9
Relative access, 12
Restore
image, 71
incremental, 72–73
with volume shadowing, 74
See also Backups

RIGHTSLIST.DAT, 52
Rights lists, 93–94
use of, 93
user groups, 93

S

Satellites, 111, 112
Security, 89–98
accounts/passwords, 90–91
alarms/audits, 96–98
login, 48–50
program privilege control, 95–96
rights lists, 93–94
user groups, 91–93
Sequential access, 12
Serial line interface protocol (SLIP), 103
SET ACCOUNTING command, 50, 53
SET AUDIT command, 96
SET DEVICE command, 57, 59
SET FILE command, 13
SET PASSWORD command, 46
SET PRINTER command, 57
SET TERMINAL command, 57, 58–59
defined, 57
in queue setup, 59
use example, 58
SHOW ACCOUNTING command, 50, 53
SHOW AUDIT command, 96–97
SHOW CLUSTER command, 115, 116
SHOW command, 15
SHOW ENTRY command, 56
SHOW ERROR command, 77–78, 87
in cluster environment, 77–78
display, 78
SHOW INTRUSION command, 97–98
SHOW MEMORY command, 79
SHOW PROCESS command, 80
SHOW PROCESS/QUOTA command, 18–19
SHOW QUEUE command, 56
SHOW SECURITY command, 92
SHOW SYSTEM command, 20, 80
Shutdown, 27–28
SHUTDOWN script, 27–28

www.ingramcontent.com/pod-product-compliance
Lightning Source LLC
Chambersburg PA
CBHW061420210326
41598CB00035B/6277